Spicestory

Spicestory

Hugh and Colleen Gantzer

Foreword:

Dr M.S. Swaminathan

NIYOGI
BOOKS

Overseas Distribution

USA and Canada
ACC Distribution
email: sales@accdistribution.com
www.accdistribution.com

United Kingdom, Ireland, Europe and Africa
Kodansha Europe Ltd.
email: info@kodansha.eu
www.kodansha.eu

Cambodia, Burma, Laos and Thailand
Paragon Asia Co. Ltd.
email: info@paragonasia.com
www.paragonasia.com

Published in association with

Published by

NIYOGI BOOKS

D-78, Okhla Industrial Area, Phase-I
New Delhi-110 020, INDIA
Tel: 91-11-26816301, 49327000
Fax: 91-11-26810483, 26813830
Email: niyogibooks@gmail.com
Website: www.niyogibooksindia.com

Authors: Hugh and Colleen Gantzer
Editor: Gita Rajan
Design: Nabanita Das

Text and those Visuals produced by the Authors © Hugh & Colleen Gantzer

ISBN: 978-93-83098-38-5
Publication: 2014

Printed at: Niyogi Offset Pvt. Ltd., New Delhi, India

CONTENTS

INTRODUCTION

"Once you get a spice
in your home, you have
it forever. Women never
throw out spices. The
Egyptians were buried with
their spices. I know which
one I'm taking with me
when I go."

-Erma Bombeck

Spices have spiced up civilisations for ages. These fragrant flora have added zing to food, zest to life, charted the lifestyles of whole races and regions, filled the coffers of nations and shaped the history of the modern world. Culinary traditions, cultural rituals, therapeutic treatises, trade and commerce, the beauty industry, the languages of the world—there is hardly a realm of life that has not been spruced up by spices.

We offer you in the pages of this book, a journey through time and space, a voyage across millennia, spanning continents and cultures all around the globe; an exotic journey that weaves a history of the world for you through the saga of spices.

The ubiquitous presence of spices has not been adequately chronicled to date. Food and lifestyle publications linger on the flavour of spices but hardly offer an insight into their history. The historians, on their part, have identified the role of spices

in yesteryears, but have precious little to comment on their prominence in today's world. Commerce has relegated them to the level of commodities, whereas the plethora of scientific papers is way beyond the reach of the common reader.

It was to fill the yawning gulf between these extremes that the Spices Board envisaged a volume that would delight and inform the specialist and the lay reader alike, give food for thought to the culinary expert and the therapist, the economist and the historian, and whet the appetite of anyone who loves reading a good story. The choice of an author for *Spicestory* was quite easy. The search for someone who had travelled extensively, relished the cuisine of countless countries and climes, someone imbued with a sound historical sense, yielded just one name—the Gantzers.

Food is the fuel that keeps the world going. As long as we cherish food that is tasty and nutritious, the spices industry will continue to remain recession-proof, unaffected as ever by any kind of economic slowdown. As 'the spice-bowl of the world,' India, the world's largest producer, consumer, and exporter of spices, has a unique position. Being the nodal organisation for this industry in India,

the Spices Board deems it essential to spread the story of spices far and wide. We take pride in dedicating it to the multitudes who star in this epic narrative – the royalty of yore, the policymakers of today, ancient navigators, the farmers, traders, exporters, scientists, chefs and everyone who cooks, serves and eats food lovingly flavoured with the goodness of spices.

You will, in the following pages, travel along the perfumed spice routes of the world, enjoy the rich aroma of spicelore, and savour the wholesome significance of spices in the world of yesterday, today, and tomorrow.

Happy reading!

Flavourfully yours,
Dr. A. Jayathilak, IAS
Chairman
Spices Board India

FOREWORD

"Variety is the spice of life" is a common saying, thereby emphasising the key role played by spices in making our life interesting.

India's heritage in spices has been a source of admiration and attraction worldwide. The present book captures this wonderful Spicestory. Dr A Jayathilak IAS, Chairman, Spices Board India ably assisted by Dr P.S. Sreekantan Thampi has traced the roots of our spice heritage to the days when Buddhist monks spread a love of spices in Tibet and China. They have entrusted Hugh and Colleen Gantzer, whose extensive travel experiences have led to the birth of many stories and anectodes relating to spices, with the task of writing the book. This wonderful couple who live in

the Himalayas were the right choice to spread the love of spices.

India's rich biodiversity in spices is also related to culinary and cultural diversity. Spices have moved from India to all countries in the world and have also become an important component of both traditional and modern medicine. The use of spices is spearheading a wellness movement. There are many books on spices but the present one also brings out the historical and spiritual values of spices. The book captures the fascinating history of spices beginning forty thousand years ago. The book covers in a most interesting manner the history of Pepper, Cinnamon, Cardamom, Cloves, Turmeric, Chillies, Mustard, Nutmeg and Mace, Cumin, Coriander, Fennel, Fenugreek, Saffron, Vanilla, Mint, and the other related spices of great value in the food and medicinal

Kathakali with Spices ,,

plant industries. There is also a short write-up on the very valuable work being done by the Spices Board India.

Thanks to the work of the Spices Board, the primacy of India in the world of spices has not only been maintained but strengthened as well.

We owe a deep debt of gratitude to the authors for preparing this remarkable book which certainly will be an important

catalyst in achieving the goal of earning US $10 billion through Spices exports.

I commend the book to all who are interested in adding spice to their life.

M S Swaminathan

An array of spices essential to the hot and fiery curries! Whole and grounded

Pages 2-3: Spices add zest and colour - *garam masala* central to Indian cooking

Page 9: Prayer wheels at the Buddhist Monastery in Sikkim (above); The Buddha too loves spices (below)

In the Beginning

A
PREVALENCE
OF
SPICES

Spices have powered civilisations, redrawn maps, influenced cultures.

Down the corridors of time we flew, tracking the prevalence of spices all through the history of mankind. We were guided by our intuitions and the research of scholars, borne on the wings of fragrances, flavours and aromatics, across countries and continents, millennia unravelling swiftly below us. Ice sheets spread and receded, seas froze revealing new land routes and still we coursed, led by the lure of spices. Then, down a column of beckoning smoke, we descended into the Zagros Mountains of Iraq. We were now forty thousand years into the past. There, below us, stood a group of stocky people with heavy brows and jaws and low foreheads, clustered around a pit. In it, one of their children had been laid to rest, his head cradled on his right hand. Beside

GREECE
Athens
Ephesus
Sardis
Constantinople
(Istanbul)
Black Sea
Danube
Volga
Ural
ANATOLIA
TURKEY
Trebizond
Erzurum
Caspian Sea
Aral Sea
WESTERN TURKESTAN
Oxus
Ferg
Lake
Antioch
Dara
Nisibis
Tabriz
Kokand
Samarkand
Alexandria
Tyre
Damascus
Palmyra
MESOPOTAMIA
Ecbatana
Rayy
Merv
Nishapur
Bactra
(Balkh)
Cairo
Gaza
Jerusalem
Baghdad
IRAQ
Ctesiphon
EGYPT
Petra
Susa
Isfahan
IRAN
Hindu Kush
Syrian Desert
Euphrates
Tigris
Apologos
Myos Hormus
Leuce Come
Nile
Medina
Persian Gulf
Hormuz
PUN
Harappa
Mohenjo-Daro
Karachi
Barbaricon
Jeddah
Mecca
ARABIAN PENINSULA
Muscat
Gulf of Oman
Baryg
(Broa
Red Sea
OMAN
IN
Salalah
Arabian sea
Malabar Coast
Muza
Aden
Cana
Zeila
Cape of Spices
Socotra
ETHIOPIA
SOMALIA
Mombasa

STEPPE

Lake Baikal

Karakorum

MONGOLIA

Gobi Desert

Urumqi

Turfan

Shan

Kucha

TARIM BASIN

Dunhuang

GANSU CORRIDOR

makan

Shang-du

Great Wall

Khanbalik (Beijing)

Shangtung Peninsula

KOREA

JAPAN

Nagasaki

Huang He (Yellow R.)

Loyang

Huai

Yellow Sea

Hang-Chou Bay

Changan (Xi'an)

PLATEAU OF TIBET

Chang Jiang (Yangtze)

CHINA

Foochow (Fuzhou)

Zaitun (Quanzhou)

Formosa (Taiwan)

PACIFIC

OCEAN

Himalaya

Brahmaputra

Canton (Guanzhou)

Ganges

Tamralipti

Cattigara (Haiphong)

Hanoi

Mekong

Vijaya

South China Sea

PHILIPPINES

Cholamandal

Madras

Bay of Bengal

Pegu

Kra Isthmus

Oc-eo

Pondichery

Anuradhapura

SRI LANKA

INDIAN OCEAN

Strait of Malacca

MALAYSIA

Melaka

Singapore

SUMATRA

BORNEO

SULAWESI

A PREVALENCE OF SPICES

him were charred bones with shreds of meat on them: food for his journey into the afterlife. The meat had a lingering, herbal aroma: it had been wrapped in leaves before being ember-baked. The tribe had relished its flavour and had gathered handfuls of the herb to add to their meals. These people were Neanderthals. Like the animals they killed, they, too, were primarily hunter-gatherers.

But they were also very different from the animals they hunted.

The bison they had slaughtered had been environment-dependent, migrating with its herd, from pasture to pasture as the seasons changed. These animals could not, in even the slightest way, control the ambiance in which they lived. The Neanderthals could. They had discovered, and domesticated, fire, and fire gave them freedom. It warmed their lives in winter, dried their coverings of skin and furs when they got wet, cured hides even when the sun was obscured by clouds. Most important, it broke down the tough tissues of bison-meat by cooking. Even children and elders could share in the feast with as much relish as the youth. Moreover, the tribe could preserve excess food by smoking it so that no one need go hungry

even when the hunters returned empty handed. And because the Neanderthals had risen above their environment they could think of the future, of an afterlife. The Neanderthals had found both a spice and a religion and those discoveries became the lasting heritage of all mankind.

We left them behind, lured by another fragrance wafting out of the future. Time unreeled, the Neanderthals had gone. Another, slimmer, more intelligent people had taken over. They looked very much like us and were called Cro-Magnon. We crawled into one of their rock-shelters in Bhimbetka. Lamps of animal-fat flickered on the uneven floor, a bare-bodied young man held aloft a flaming torch. A shaman-

artist worked, bent down occasionally to charge his vision with deep inhalations of the strong incense rising from a pot of slowly smouldering ginger, fennel, cinnamon, resins and aromatic leaves. He was painting a hunting scene on the walls of the shelter. He and his people believed that what he painted would actually happen. The smoke that he breathed into himself would stimulate his mind, create that great sympathetic magic.

Even in these very early days of mankind's development, herbs, spices and aromatics had acquired a magical-medicinal aura.

Still questing through history for our Spicestory we sped forward, 4,600 years before our time, and spiralled down to Egypt. Thousands of men were toiling in the desert on the banks of the Nile. There was a strong aroma of sweat and pungent spices. The great pharaoh had decreed that his labourers should eat huge quantities of onions and garlic to preserve their health while they worked on building his towering memorial to immortality. It was the age of the Great Pyramids, those incredible structures raised in a vain defiance of death. Massive monuments, however, were not enough for the divine rulers of Egypt. Their bodies had to be uncorrupted when

A PREVALENCE OF SPICES

they entered the afterlife, embalmed and eternally fragrant. Huge quantities of spices such as cumin, anise, and cassia went, quite literally, into the pharaohs. Speeding ahead to 1485 BC we gazed down at a flotilla of the square-sailed ships of Queen Hatshepsut bringing back incense trees, cinnamon and other treasures from the mysterious 'land of Punt.'

The ships of Pharaonic Egypt were not built for long ocean voyages but those of their successors, the dhows of the Arabs, were sturdy ocean-going vessels. The Arabs had also discovered a cyclic storm. It blew from the west to the east from April to October, and east to west from October with a slackening off at both ends. They could not have asked for more

favourable winds, as regular as the change of seasons. So they called it 'The Season': *mausum* which, over the years, became The Monsoon.

From our elevated perch, high above the Arabian Sea, we saw determined fleets of dhows cross and return, their sails billowing with the rain-laden winds. We also observed them off-loading their cargo of spices to fellow Arab caravanners to be galumphed overland on camels through the fabulous ravine-and-cliff city of Petra. These astute Arab middlemen protected their interests by keeping the location of Petra secret, and by crafting fabulous tales about fantastic beasts who guarded these spices, to account for the exorbitant prices they demanded.

Armies of toiling Egyptian workers were fortified by Garlic

Facing page:
Jordan's iconic Petra prospered on spice caravans from India

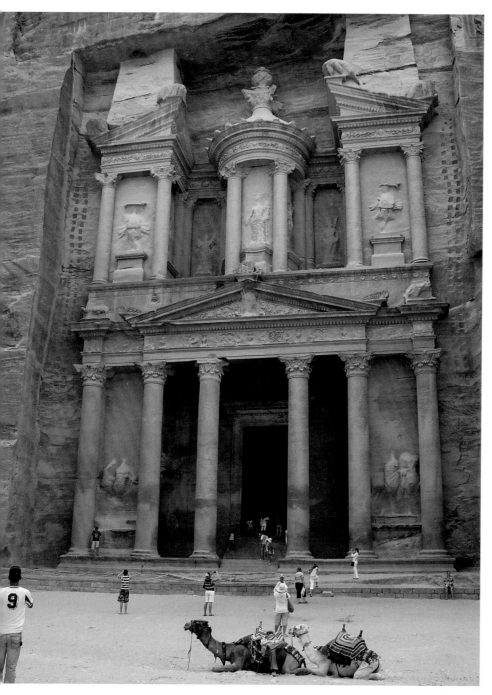

Then, in the middle of the 1st century AD, a Greek trader named Hippalus discovered the well-kept Arab secret of the Monsoons. This spurred the Romans to build stronger ships and set up a garrison in Kerala's Muziris to curb the Arabian traders. They could now make the round trip from the Red Sea to Malabar and back in a year and avoid using the overland route controlled by the Arabs. But though depleted by Roman competition, Arab dhows were still plying and so a Jewish architect named Thomas Didymus hitched a ride on an Arab spice ship. Presumably he could not risk sailing on a Roman ship because he was a follower of a man who had been crucified as a criminal by the Romans. Thomas had been ordered by Jesus Christ to carry the message of Christianity to India. True to his master's orders, Thomas established one of the oldest, surviving, Christian churches in the world in the heart of India's spice lands: Kerala. Centuries later, a follower of the Prophet Mohammed also sailed in from Arabia on a spice ship. His name was Malik Ibn Dinar. Christianity and Islam had reached India following the Spice Trail.

Inevitably, the interests of both faiths were poised for conflict across the known world. Then, to add to the misery of

A PREVALENCE OF SPICES

Europe, we saw hordes of lice-carrying rats scampering ashore from ships and spreading disease. The Plague, called the Black Death, raged like a wildfire through the teeming and noisome streets of the continent. We looked down in horror as teams of corpse-carriers trundled their barrows down the cobbled, refuse-choked, lanes crying 'Bring us your dead', dragging away their pathetic loads, dumping them into mass graves before they, themselves, succumbed to the dreaded groin and armpit swellings of the disease. Even now, however, in the midst of this dreadful epidemic, physicians relied on the magical properties of spices. They wrapped themselves from head to toe in clothes filled with sachets of spices and herbs and breathed through beak-like filters stuffed with aromatics. But all around them, the common people lived in incredible squalor. Offal and human waste were thrown on the streets. Meat tended to putrefy fast because there was no way to preserve it so people had to rely on spices to disguise its stench.

Cumulative misery is a breeding ground for war. Long-standing enmities festered and burst. As the world and time spun under us the Cross and the Crescent clashed on the great battlegrounds of the Crusades. At the end of it all, however, the European nations had benefited by

Islam arrived in Asia on Arab dhows, set up the first mosque; Kerala's Cheruman Perumal Masjid

their exposure to the aesthetic tastes of the Islamic civilisation. We saw the merchants of Venice, Genoa and Pisa grow fat and prosperous on the new burgeoning demand for spices from the East. But only the rich could afford to buy these expensive condiments and the gap between the haves and the have-nots was widening. The majority of Europeans still lived in deplorable conditions. In time their sullen anguish began to disturb their rulers.

We were now in the 15th century. The Roman Empire had gone and the Arab dominance of the spice trade had reasserted itself causing spice prices to soar again. From our vantage point above time and space, we noticed a seething ferment down below. Europe had started to buzz like a hive of angry wasps. Rulers, traders, seafarers sailed out from Portugal, Spain, Holland and England on desperate voyages to break the Arabs' renewed stranglehold on the spice trade, particularly the pepper trade with India. Many of these explorers lost their way in dangerous, and uncharted, seas, but they often ended up discovering new lands for their nations. In 1497-98, Henry VII of England couldn't find anyone in his kingdom willing to risk such a hazardous voyage of discovery. He finally

Searching for an Atlantic spice route to India, Christopher Colombus discovered America for Spain. Icons of the kingdoms of Spain carry his coffin in a Spanish cathedral

commissioned the Italian sailor Giovanni Caboto. He didn't discover the sea route to India but he did explore Newfoundland, the Gulf of St Lawrence and the coasts of Greenland and Labrador adding to the terrains controlled by Britain. The king was delighted and, from then on, the Brits have referred to the Italian as 'John Cabot'. Interestingly, wherever these European explorers stepped on a strange shore and met unknown people they thought they'd discovered their own route to India. Consequently places and people were misnamed the West Indies, 'Red Indians' and Amerindians. Thanks to the quest for Indian spices, the known world grew in what has been called The Age of

A PREVALENCE OF SPICES

Exploration. From this 'New World' came yams, kidney beans, maize, tapioca, tobacco, chocolate and the hammock. Spice seekers had changed the world.

That, however, was just the beginning. Great social upheavals followed: too many for us to discern from our high vantage point above the swirling kaleidoscope of history.

We did, however, perceive that the plundered wealth of the captive nations filled the coffers of the colonial powers and their ethnic clones, eventually financing the much-vaunted Industrial Revolution. Out of the *hubris*, the exaggerated pride and bloated self-confidence, that these purloined riches had created, were born the World Wars. Gazing down at those bloody conflicts we saw that every one of the initial battling nations had been a colonial power except Japan, and Japan had made no secret of its desire to join the colonial club under the guise of the, so-called, 'Asian Co-prosperity Sphere.' It was fitting that, two years after World War II ended, India led the demolition of the colonial regimes around the world. The land that had started the Great Spice Race was the flag-bearer of a world-spanning freedom movement that has done much to jettison the more disagreeable consequences of that commercial quest for the spices of India.

With that we can close a chapter that began about forty thousand years ago in the Zagros Mountains of Iraq and take a close look at the spices that have, throughout the ages, nurtured the seeds of our civilisation.

Pepper, the spice that lured Europe to India, the spiceland

The Berry that Launched a Thousand Ships

PEPPER

PEPPER

The music crashed around us: trumpets, drums, cymbals, a thundering martial blast.

It was jarring, unexpected. We had settled down to dinner in a small, quiet, restaurant, in the small, quiet, Swiss town of Vevey, when the doors of the kitchen were flung open, sound blared out, the chef emerged in a World War II tin helmet and bearing aloft a large Swiss flag. He was followed by the owner wearing a policeman's cap and shouldering a huge, wooden, cylinder which looked like a missile launcher. Everyone froze. The troopers stomped up to a table, saluted, pointed the weapon at the centre, and activated it. Pepper ground out of the great caster and spread evenly on the cheese melting gently on its spirit burner.

Our relief was palpable. We beamed and clapped and the chef and the owner marched triumphantly into the kitchen as the martial music stopped and Swiss serenity returned to *Les Trois Sifflets*. It was the restaurant's dramatic welcome given to all customers who ordered fondue: that atypical Swiss dish eaten with chunks of bread dipped in the liquefied cheese.

Much later, we asked a foodie friend, "Is the pepper necessary? We don't sprinkle pepper on our cheese at home."

Her eyebrows shot up to her hairline in surprise. "Ah, but how could you have fondue without pepper? It is like … like …" she seemed to be at a loss for words, "… caviar without champagne!"

"So what did the Swiss do before the Romans discovered Kerala?" we asked.

Above: In the 16th century, cylindrical Pepper-boxes with perforated lids were fashionable. Then Victorian potters created Pepper Shakers resembling characters from Charles Dickens' books. Wooden Pepper Grinders are now favoured and in Switzerland a restaurateur wielded a grinder the size of a bazooka to sprinkle fresh pepper on fondue

Right: Around Lake Geneva, Switzerland

PEPPER

She gave us a deadpan look. "Before that, my friends, there was no Switzerland!"

Our minds skipped and stretched over the world's sustained *affaire* with the black berry of Malabar. The Romans who, at one time, held the whole of the known world under their command, were obsessed with great eating orgies and they believed that pepper helped them to settle the effects of excessive gorging. To protect their interests and their digestions, they had based a legion in Kerala's Muziris in the hope that their cohorts would curb the burgeoning greed of Arab middlemen. This did lower the prices of pepper in Rome, but it only increased the Romans' hunger for the spice. And so when the Germanic Visigoth king, Alaric, besieged Rome he demanded gold and three thousand pounds of peppercorns to lift the siege. The Romans found it fairly easy to raise the gold but they had a hard time collecting the pepper: they had eaten most of their stock! They did, eventually, manage but that only offered a temporary relief. Alaric returned but that is not part of our Spicestory.

Meanwhile, the virtues of pepper had spread all over the Roman world and into the myriad tongues of their subjects. It became a generic name for spice. Spice merchants were called, *Pfeffersacke* in Germany … giving rise to the surname Pfeffer … *Poivriers* in France and *Pepperers* in England.

Pepper had also become a very valuable commodity in England and landlords often insisted that their tenants pay their rents in peppercorns. It became part of the local idiom. Pep is a noun for brisk energy and high spirits. Pepper is a verb which means to hit with repeated rapid blows, to shower with shots, and to

sprinkle or cover with as in the phrase 'the report was peppered with statistics' or 'her face was peppered with freckles' It even taught children how to pronounce their words in the tongue-twisting nursery rhyme:

Peter Piper picked a peck of pickled pepper;
A peck of pickled pepper Peter Piper picked;
If Peter Piper picked a peck of pickled pepper,
Where's the peck of pickled pepper Peter Piper picked?

That's from an old book entitled *Peter Piper's Practical Principles of Plain and Perfect Pronunciation.* It's still used by speech trainers to assist stutterers.

Then there are the phrases 'To pepper one well' meaning to give someone a thrashing. *Peppercorn rent* is now the term for a nominal payment but was once a description of an exorbitant one because pepper was then an extremely expensive spice, thanks to the excessive mark-ups imposed by Arab middlemen.

We've told the story about how the growing demands of the Arab traders compelled the European kingdoms to launch their own voyages to discover a sea route to the spice lands, particularly to the legendary pepper lands of India. But there are interesting sub-plots to that tale. For one thing pepper was a homestead crop, not a plantation one. Individual families grew their own pepper vines up trees in their backyard for their own needs which, in Kerala at least, seemed to be for home remedies. We have not, as yet, been able to find an authentic old Malayali dish which listed pepper as an ingredient. The berry did find a place in traditional Ayurvedic formulations according to some practitioners of this ancient medical system. This probably accounts for the fact that pepper was an accepted gift to the powerful goddess in the great temple in Cranganore, not far from Muziris. One reason for this is that many of the devi's devotees believed that when the goddess visited a home her powerful presence caused one of the family to break out in

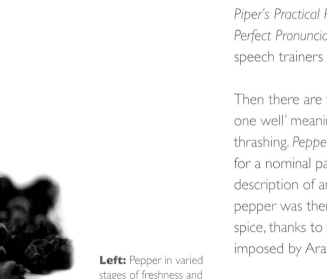

Left: Pepper in varied stages of freshness and drying—green, yellow, red and finally black or white

Above right: Green berries waiting to be harvested

PEPPER

small, black, eruptions like peppercorns. Modern doctors call it small pox and have virtually eradicated it from India by a sustained campaign of inoculations. It is also more than likely that folk medicine used peppercorns based on the principle that *'like cures like'*. Whatever the reason may be, however, the fact is that the *devi* temple in Cranganore became a great entrepot of peppercorns drawing wholesale traders from around the world.

This is why the Portuguese admiral, Vasco da Gama, was ordered to find a sea route to India *'for Pepper and Christ'*, in that order: commerce first, then faith. He and his successors were disappointed to find that there were Christians in Kerala who had been followers of Christ for many centuries before his own people in Portugal. The Syrian Christians of Kerala trace their faith back to the arrival of one of the chosen disciples of Christ, St Thomas, who landed in Cranganore in AD 52, a fact recognised by the Government of India who have issued two postage stamps to commemorate this historic event. He sailed in on a spice trader's ship and established seven and a half churches in Kerala in seven pepper trading stations and one pepper buying depot, according to traditional belief.

Keeping first things first, however, da Gama donned his plumes and Admiral's uniform and, accompanied by his glittering retinue, marched proudly into the presence of the Zamorin, the ruler of Malabar. He wanted permission to buy pepper, set up a trading post on the coast, and carry back some saplings of the valuable pepper vine. The Zamorin, by all accounts, was more amused than impressed by the Portuguese Admiral and his fidalgos. They seemed to him to be overdressed popinjays, strutting and sweating in his warm and humid kingdom. He was also, however, an astute

Offerings of Pepper to the Goddess made the Devi temple into an international entrepot of this cottage-grown spice

Facing page: The altar of the Church in Cranganore marking the spot where St Thomas landed in India, sailing in on a spice ship

PEPPER

A Pepper plucker
harvests berries

Facing page:
Workers busy
harvesting pepper

Pages 32-33: Vasco
da Gama meets the
unimpressed Zamorin

monarch, and he was ready to trade with the *firangs*. But when his ministers learnt that he was also prepared to let the foreigners have pepper plants they advised him against losing their monopoly. The Zamorin is said to have reassured them by saying, "They can have the plants, but they don't have the favourable climate of Kerala." He was wrong. The former Portuguese colony of Brazil does have the same warm and humid environment as Kerala and, today, they are still a significant producer of pepper.

The pepper vine needs shade, a support to climb on, such as a tree or a scaffolding, rain and heat. It ascends to a height of eight metres but is generally kept pruned to a more manageable height. The berries are green, at first, then they darken to yellow and finally to red. Pepper farming is labour-intensive because the berries have to be manually harvested: the unripe, green, ones to be converted into black pepper by drying, the slightly more mature, greenish yellow, ones to become the milder-tasting white pepper after their outer coverings are removed. New vines are cultivated from the fleshy, rooted, upper cuttings of vines: pepper vines cling to their supports by sending out small roots along their stems. These

PEPPER

Above: Pepper vines rise like green pillars

Left: On their vines, Pepper berries hang like green pendants

Facing page: Harvested Pepper berries are dried on mats in the warm tropical sun (left); Berries on Pepper vines ripen from green through yellow to red (right above)

rootlets serve both as supports and as the 'mouths' of the plant drawing sustenance from the moss, moisture and wind-blown humus that might have collected on their supports. They can, thus, easily become the main nutrition providers of the new vines when they are planted in the ground.

The success of the Portuguese in the pepper business had set off a tsunami of unease through the spice trading countries of Europe. They decided to establish their own centres in India and formed their own East India Companies. This led to turf wars between the traders in the spice lands of the world, eventually sucking their countries into these conflicts. In India the odds should have been stacked in favour of the larger nations: Portugal, Holland and France. But the skilled *realpolitik* of the English paid

A wooden hand-grinder converts black and white pepper into aromatic seasoning

"

PEPPER

off and, before long, the pepper-trading East India Company became the greatest power in India, ruling vast areas of the sub-continent. Their success encouraged the establishment of the other European colonies across the world.

The quest for pepper had started a cultural chain reaction around the globe. The languages and mores of England, Spain, France, Portugal, Holland, Germany and even Denmark influenced and merged with those of other people. The seemingly inexhaustible demand for pepper had led to an ever widening interest in other spices and the consequent reaching out to other lands and people all across time and the continents.

One of these other spices had been a favourite of apothecaries and perfumers for many centuries but was now in demand as a new flavour. Unlike pepper it was not a berry but a fragrant bark from the same tropical lands.

Greenish-yellow berries, with their husks removed, become the mild White Pepper

Nest of the Phoenix

CINNAMON

CINNAMON

This one's straight out of the *Arabian Nights*.

According to one version of the old Arab traders' tale:

'In the middle of a distant, savage, land there is a great lake filled with awesome creatures. But none are so awesome as the one that lives on an island atop high cliffs. There, when the time is ripe, this flying creature builds its nest, clinging to the precipitous precipices. But in this nest, this creature lays no eggs: it has no eggs. In fact there are no males and females of its species. It exists alone. And so when it feels itself growing old, it flies deep into the forest, finds a special grove of scented trees, strips the bark of those wondrous trees, and builds its nest. Then, when the nest is ready, it sits therein, flaps its golden wings rapidly and causes the fragrant bark of its nest to burn with a scorching flame that reduces that fabulous bird to ashes. Thus, out of those glowing ashes, a new creature emerges. This creature is known as the self-renewing Phoenix.

And so you see, my friend, it is very dangerous to scale the cliff, rob the magical bark and return before the Phoenix returns. That is why cinnamon is so very expensive …'

But expensive or not, this delectable spice was in great demand from the days of the Pharaohs of ancient Egypt. Earlier, however, it was revered as an almost magical aromatic, held in awe for its perfume credited with the power to ward off the evils of disease and decay. It was

Cinnamon quills and powder

Above: A close-up of the Pyramid of Giza, Egypt. The stones lying in front add to the ambiance

A spice trader in Aswan, Egypt. Arab spice merchants created spicy tales linking Cinnamon with the fabulous Phoenix

probably this belief that the perceptive Arabs exploited as our 21st century advertising agencies exploit our belief that 'Fair is Lovely'. That ancient cinnamon promotion was a major success story: it created both desirability and exclusivity and, therefore, a need. The Pharaonic VIPs of Egypt wanted this magic bark because, if it could rejuvenate the Phoenix, it would certainly restore their youthful good looks when they were embalmed for their long journey into the afterlife. This belief probably influenced the mad emperor, Nero, when he ordered all the cinnamon

CINNAMON

in Rome to be burnt so that its perfumed smoke would accompany his dead wife's corpse on its last rites. The word *perfume* means *'through smoke.'*

Attractive aromas are the distinctive quality of all spices, herbs and aromatics. Their initial appeal lies in their oleoresins. We had an interesting conversation with a friend, an MIT man, who has specialised in the commercial uses of spices and is a Director of one of the leading spice companies in India. We speculated … and this is still just a speculation … that since the strongest resins used as incense come from thorny trees and shrubs growing in harsh desert environments, such gums must boost the plants' chances of survival. Their armoury of thorns would deter animals from grazing on them but their main enemies are sap-sucking insects who can get through their defensive spikes. The strong oleoresins serve as a second line of defence. This is also why such gums as frankincense, myrrh, camphor, sandalwood and cinnamon are used in religious ceremonies attended by large congregations. They not only compensate for body odours but they also disinfect and fumigate the premises where people have assembled. Fumigation was also an essential part of the Egyptian embalming process. Later, the Romans, with their uninhibited private lives, made excessive use of perfumes including chewing cinnamon as a breath sweetener. This, possibly, gave it the additional appeal as a reputed aphrodisiac.

It is clear, therefore, that cinnamon was first used as an aromatic in rituals and assemblies, not as a condiment in cuisine.

The earliest mention of cinnamon being used as a condiment is in AD 716 when an emperor of the Franks gave cinnamon to a monastery in Normandy. The monks in monasteries, however, were also physicians who maintained herb gardens to use in their medical preparations. So in Normandy, too, cinnamon might have been used by their apothecaries and not as an ingredient in their food. A century

Cinnamon and Cassia sticks in the form seen in provision shops in Indian towns

later we do find that the cooks in a Swiss monastery in St Gall used cinnamon to season fish. After that, however, there is a crashing historical silence till the *Ain-i-Akbari* written by Abul Fazl, Prime Minister to the Mughal Emperor Akbar, in the 16th century. There he lists cinnamon as the ingredient in a number of dishes prepared by the royal chefs.

It is most likely, therefore, that it was the Mughals who introduced cinnamon as an ingredient in *garam masala,* that essential mixture of spices that finds pride of place in most Indian kitchens today.

But, then, who was the innovative chef or baker who had the courage to use this traditionally medicinal spice in European cuisine? We have savoured it on cakes and pastries in virtually every country in Europe. There, however, unlike the way we use it in India, it is always added to give a little zest to desserts and confectionery, possibly on snacks like cinnamon toast, but never in the main meal. The most unusual use of cinnamon that we've experienced in a European country was when we sat in the *Cacao Sampaka,* a chocolate bar, in Madrid. Our mugs of rich cocoa were served to us

In Spain's Madrid, the *Cacao Sampaka* offers steaming mugs of chocolate with Cinnamon quills to stir and chew

CINNAMON

steaming and with quills of cinnamon
to stir the beverage and chew upon. It
gave a very intriguing flavour to the hot
chocolate and if chocolate bars ever
become popular in our land cinnamon
sticks would make an interesting addition.
At that time we wanted to ask who had
introduced this unusual way of flavouring
chocolate. We have only just learnt that,
in Mexico, cinnamon is popular in the
brewing of hot chocolate. This led to a
fascinating line of thought.

Chocolate was brought to Europe by
the Spanish conquistadores returning
after plundering the riches of South
America. Did the people of those tropical
lands use a local variety of cinnamon
to flavour their beverage? And was that
taste passed down to their ethnic and
cultural descendants in Mexico? We have
put that query on hold till we get more
information on this fascinating byway
of Spicestory.

To return to our time, we have referred
to the cinnamon served to us in that
Spanish chocolate bar as both 'quills' and
'sticks'. Quills are the correct technical
name, but sticks are what they look
like though they are not sticks of the
cinnamon tree. In fact they might not be

Cassia and Cinnamon
sticks being laid out in
trays for drying

Above: Cinnamon
quills ready to be used

A Cinnamon tree

cinnamon but its cousin, cassia. To further confuse the issue, while Britain makes a difference between *Cinnamomum zeylanicum,* which it regards as the real cinnamon, and *cassia,* its 'poor relative', the US, however, makes no such class distinction. In fact, very often the price of cassia is higher than that of cinnamon. And the chances are that the cinnamon you buy from the shop in your neighbourhood is cassia.

Cinnamon grows in our southern states so it seems strange that it did not become part of Indian food before the Mughals arrived in India. Cassia prefers the eastern Himalayas. Since, nowadays, both are used in rituals they could have acquired a certain sacred character which might have inhibited their use in cooking. The Mughals, whose culture had Chinese underpinnings,

CINNAMON

had no such inhibitions. They could well have introduced the home remedy known to many Indian families including our own. In a cup of warm water, we mix a spoonful of honey and a teaspoon of powdered cinnamon. It reputedly 'clears the blood of all impurities' which is one way of saying that it also lowers the cholesterol levels. It has worked for those of our family who have used it but do check it out with your physician before you try it. Incidentally, neither our ancestors, nor the Mughals, distinguished between cinnamon and cassia.

Not that there is much of a difference. Both cinnamon and cassia are evergreens of the laurel family, a relationship which they share with camphor. If allowed to grow they could rise to over ten metres but, like the tea tree, they are cut back to become bushes. Each bush is carefully pruned to leave six to eight branches. Two years later, when these branches have reached a height of two metres or so, they are cut to ground level during the rainy season. After three years, new shoots should appear which can then be harvested.

Using special sickle-shaped knives the bark is peeled off the shoots, tied in bundles,

The bark is peeled from the branches. This is done skillfully to get long strips. The inner bark is then carefully separated from the coarse outer bark and left to dry as quills or sticks

Page 48: Cinnamon being harvested. The branches are chopped down and cut

Page 48-49: Arab and Eastern traders monopolised the Spice trade

CINNAMON

coarser, its taste more assertive but it has one qualification above that of its seemingly superior cousin. It is mentioned in the Chinese *Ch'u Ssu (Elegies of Ch'u)* penned as far back as the 4th century BC. In that ancient document cassia is described as an ingredient to flavour food. That makes it one of the oldest condiments used by man.

Which brings us to the second spice that goes into our *garam masala*. It makes a very sexist demand on its farmers and, if that need is not met, it will sulk and not produce its aromatic seeds. This is why we draw on the *Arabian Nights* again and think of it as the, very feminine, Scheherazade spice.

and left to ferment for a day. Then, very carefully, the outer bark is removed leaving the light-coloured inner bark to dry in the shade and then in the sun for three or four days. This bark then curls into itself to form quills. Smaller quills are then inserted into larger quills to form metre-long 'pipes'. This is the best cinnamon and it has a curious grading: 00000. That's three zeros more than James Bond. The bits of the inner bark that have fallen off during the quilling-piping process are collected and have their own grades.

Cassia goes through much the same process as cinnamon. Its quills are a little

Cinnamon Oil
extracted from the
tree is a high value
end-product

The Scheherazade Seed

CARDAMOM

The planter was embarrassed.

When we asked him, "What are those women doing?" his eyes flicked away from us and he mumbled, "They are ... er ... they're harvesting cardamom." We had driven out of the commercial capital of Kerala state, Cochin now called Kochi, and into the wooded mountains of the Western Ghats. We had parked our car in a part of this forested range known, appropriately, as the Cardamom Hills. In a shaded valley, giant trees soared into the sky, their canopies basking in the sun, their feet in deep shadow. In that verdant gloom grew huge clumps of lily-like plants, their leaves flaring up to four metres high. Women in bright saris crouched on the forest floor, touching the capsule-bearing stems sprouting out of the base of each bush. We looked

closely at what they were doing and then turned to the young planter.

"Not all of them are plucking the pods," we said. "Some are only touching the flowers. Why are they doing that?"

He smiled sheepishly. "Yes they are ... some of them are touching the flowers. If they don't ... if a woman does not touch them, if a man does ... then ..." he still seemed reluctant to go on as if it was something he was ashamed of, and then he blurted out, "... if a woman does not touch the flowers, they might not form seeds." He shrugged and decided to be frank. "There are many strange things about cardamom. Another thing is that it is difficult to

Harvested green Cardamom

Above: Cardamom plant thrives with a woman's touch

Right: A cheerful Cardamom(large black) plucker with her cane basket

CARDAMOM

domesticate it, to tame it. If you take it out of its deep forest environment it is most unhappy. It is easiest for us to give in and cultivate it where it wants to be even though the clumps have to be grown so close together that mechanical harvesting becomes almost impossible. We have to send our pickers in to manoeuvre their way between the clumps."

It all seemed very unlikely, as if a PR person had spun a promotional yarn to boost the product. The astute Arabs had done it centuries ago to inflate the price of cinnamon, another ingredient in our cuisine's *garam masala.*

Back home in the Himalayas, we had browsed through our reference library. There was nothing about the fertilising hand of women needed to enhance the setting of seed-filled cardamom pods. Perhaps it was a local phenomenon, unique to the women of Kerala. Or perhaps, the cardamom farmers in Guatemala, where they also grow this aromatic spice, were prepared to accept a lower yield. It is a fact that cardamom is a native of the Western Ghats and Kerala leads the world in its production. We put aside the touchy-feely aspect as

CARDAMOM

an interesting facet of our research and moved on.

Ahead of us, on that shadow-dappled road, a blue haze hung over a cleared patch of hillside. There was the acrid smell of a bonfire. As we drew near we saw wood fires burning under large metal sheets. The sheets had been piled with the rich, dark, humus of the forest. The planter told us that soil was being prepared for nursery beds. Heat and the fumes of burning logs would rid the loam of nematode worms and other pests like fungus. In this disinfected soil, cardamom seed would be planted immediately after picking. There they would be nurtured, cosseted from direct sun, the soil of the beds kept damp but never too wet, weeded, sprayed with disinfectants. After a year of tender, loving, care the strongest seedlings would be transplanted into secondary beds and then they would be planted in their final home.

The planter referred to the forests where the cardamom bushes would mature, and start yielding pods, as 'fields'. But that was a technical term borrowed from more domesticated crops like rice and wheat. There was nothing tamed about these 'fields.'

"For thousands of years" the planter said, "until about 1800, forest tribes and intrepid plainsmen hacked their way through these jungles, braving wild animals and dangerous snakes … this is the home of the great King Cobra … blood-sucking leeches and, worst of all, the dreaded anopheles mosquito whose females carry the malaria parasite. Then, by trial and error, we learnt how to cultivate cardamom. Come, I'll show you a cardamom field being prepared."

We drove on. Thunder rumbled, there was a flash of lightning, and sheets of rain slathered down blurring our windscreen

Page 56: Women cleaning green cardamom (both)

Page 57: Large, Black, Cardamom thrives in the lush forested hills of the North-East

A field of large, Black, Cardamom

like a thick smear of oil. Then, as suddenly as it had come, it stopped. The sun came out beaming brightly, varnishing the leaves of the forest. There was the rich after-rain aroma of mushrooms. Around us, under the tall, dripping, evergreens, jungle knives flashed and slashed in the hands of bare-bodied, sweating men. They were clearing away the undergrowth, ensuring that the cardamom would not lose out to voracious competitors. Later, just before dark monsoon clouds swept over Kerala, pits would be dug for the strong plants from the secondary beds. If all went well, and there was just the right amount of rain and shade at the right time, and the parasites were kept at bay in this rich, wild, environment, the cardamom bushes would send out their panicle stalks carrying tiny flowers in April and May.

"Capsules from the flowers ripen slowly over six months from August to February," the

A farmer tending his Cardamom (large black) plant

Cardamom plants
and their fruiting
panicles carpet
the floor. Inset
of a questing
bee pollinating a
cardamom flower

CARDAMOM

planter explained. "During this critical period, teams of women visit every bush every twenty to forty days, as you saw them doing. They touch every panicle and pluck only the capsules pregnant with seeds." The pods are then washed and dried. The seeds account for about 60 per cent of the weight of the pods and, in India, we prefer to buy the pods and shell them just before use because we believe that some of the delicate aroma of the seeds evaporates after they are freed from their protective capsules.

As might have been expected the fragrance of cardamom was used to perfume the sacred fire of traditional Indic marriage ceremonies. Traditionally, cardamom had three virtues that made it a very festive spice. It was believed to aid digestion and was, consequently, very popular with Romans who indulged in gargantuan eating orgies filled with exotic dishes like larks' tongues and far more unmentionable things. It was also regarded as an aphrodisiac which was a useful additive because the eating-meetings often evolved into what a latter-day Roman called bunga-bunga parties. Thirdly, there was the very pragmatic quality of cardamom that it sweetened the breath. After all that compulsive

gormandising, the diners' breaths must have had all the qualities of a barbecue in a garbage dump!

On a more agreeable note, the northern European countries seem to have taken to this very southern Indian spice in a big way. During a tour of Finland we were served delectable little cakes with coffee. Their cardamom flavour went well with the beverage and we learnt, much later, that they are called *kaffebrod* or coffee-bread, also popular in Norway. Their neighbours, the Swedes, have a cardamom

In the shade of the forest floor, in the coastal state of Kerala, a Cardamom flower blooms

tradition associated with Christmas. One festive season we visited the home of a Swedish couple and they offered us what she referred to as *glogg*. We know that grog is a drink of rum and hot water, once served to sailors of the British Royal Navy. We thought that our blonde hostess was mispronouncing the word. She wasn't. *Glogg*, we discovered to our great delight, was a hot, cardamom-spiced, wine and one of us enjoyed it so much that we even forgot to ask for its recipe. We know, however, that the word is taken from the Swedish *glodga* which means to mull or burn.

This association of cardamom with heat has spread across many cultures, particularly the Islamic ones though, there, there is often a slight contradiction in terms. Cardamom is an essential ingredient of the Arabian *gahwa*: cardamom-coffee. It is served out of long, curve-spouted and very graceful, coffee pots. In many of their traditional societies it has to be served to all guests: not to do so would give great offence. It often has far more brewed cardamom than coffee. According to European writers, it is drunk because it is supposed to cool the system in their hot

In a Bedouin encampment in Jordan's Wadi Rum, guests are entertained with *gahwa*, Cardamom Coffee, brewed on an open hearth

Cardamom is
invariably added to
the famous Indian
masala tea "

CARDAMOM

climate but then, oddly, it is also believed to stir the libido. Perhaps the heat tends to make one lethargic and cardamom wakes one up and revives an interest in life and its zestful pleasures. We recalled the erotic Arabian classic, *The Perfumed Garden,* in which cardamom's stimulating qualities are often referred to.

This could also be the logic behind the creation of the *eladhany.* Strolling around a bazaar in Kashmir's Srinagar we spotted a silver-smith's shop with a glittering array of unusual jewellery. The venerable old artisan, sitting inside, told us that his shop was largely patronised by the gypsy Gujar herds-people.

We picked up an intriguingly fashioned piece. "Is this a locket?" we asked him.

He smiled. "You might say that. But it is not worn round the neck. The bride wears it on her wrist." He took off the stopper from the heart-shaped, filigree container. "It will hold the first food she feeds to her bridegroom: very good for both of them."

"Sweets?"

"Oh no," the white bearded man said. "It is cardamom, naturally!"

Years later we came across other Islamic wedding jewellery in a remote tribal village in Gujarat. There, however, the spice wasn't cardamom but one named after its resemblance to sharp little nails even though it really is a very benign and comforting spice. Sadly, its soaring popularity in Europe, at one time, led to cut-throat competition and a reign of terror in the gentle monsoon islands where it grew.

Above: Cardamom flower

Left: In India Cardamom pod is used as a mouth freshener or after-mint after a delicious meal

The Buds of Contention

CLOVES

Great-Grandma … we always dropped the 'Great' … loved cloves.

She had a clove in her mouth all through the day even though Grandad associated them with toothaches. Clove oil was a specific for aching teeth before high-profile toothpastes were concocted. And so Granny, who had not had a painful tooth in her adult life until she started growing a new set when she was in her seventies, had to be content with hanging her clove-studded pomander balls in her Burma teak wardrobe. "There is no need for your grandfather to open my wardrobe as there is no need for me to visit his sports rack with his guns, fishing tackle and the smell of oil, Vaseline and waders." Then she would nod her head and add, "After all, my ancestors were in Amboyna when the dirty Brits accused them of '*Massacring*' their

criminal traders who wanted to grab our clove business."

There's a lot of history, geography, sociology and economics in that statement. Grandma's family had settled in the Dutch colony of Amboyna in the Moluccas. Cloves were a major export of this island and the first ship to circumnavigate the globe, the Spaniard Ferdinand Magellan's *Victoria,* called on Amboyna before ending her world-encircling voyage in Seville with a cargo of cloves! It was on Amboyna Island, too, that the Dutch governor, trying to monopolise the world trade in cloves, ordered the felling of all clove trees growing outside the island. Many of those trees had been dedicated by the

Above: A close up of Clove buds on the branch

Right: The popular *Medievo* spice shop in Spain's Granada. The suit of armour in the foreground gives the impression that spices entered Spain through the Crusaders' contact with the Arabs

The range of spices, including Cloves used in Spanish cuisine is the widest we have seen in any European country. The basket of *Curry* speaks of an Indo-Iberian connection. Portugal, with its colonies in India, was ruled by Spain from 1580 to 1640 exposing it to the richness of Indian spices "

CLOVES

local people to their children and were believed to influence the health of the growing infant. The grossly insensitive act of killing those protected clove trees anguished the indigenous population. The Dutch governor, in a typically colonial blinkered view of the world, believed that the traders of the English East India Company had fanned this unrest because they wanted a slice of the clove trade. He ordered them arrested, tortured, and executed. Back in England this was loudly condemned as the *Amboyna Massacre*. Inevitably, the Anglo-Dutch Wars followed.

That's when Granny's Dutch ancestors left Amboyna and settled in their Indian colony of Chinsuria on the Hooghly. Granny then married Grandad from the neighbouring Danish colony of Serampore where a whole street had been named after them. And she continued to detest the 'dirty Brits'.

Clearly, even from those very early days, the little spice was weaving a tangled web through our lives. Granny, however, took a very positive view of the seemingly abrasive issue of cloves. "Yes, I've kept my pomander balls and our marriage," she would advise anyone who

cared to listen. "Remember that every successful marriage has a single, small, contentious issue. It's that touch of spice that keeps the marriage alive. Without it, as the Bard said, *life is bound in shallows and in misery.*" She had misquoted Shakespeare, of course, but it was most appropriate, nevertheless.

In fact, long before Grandma G. dispensed this piquant gem of wisdom, our people in ancient India were chewing cloves wrapped in betel leaves to sweeten their breath. This socially agreeable practice probably percolated to China, centuries later. In the 3rd century BC courtiers of the

Spices used in the
garam masala

Han court were forbidden to address their emperor unless they had fragrant cloves in their mouths.

While it is clear that cloves were popular in India and China from long before the start of the Christian era, we initially had no idea when the clove plant was introduced into our land, and by whom. A 15th century Russian traveller, writing about the port of Calicut, claimed that '*the country produces ... cloves.*' But since Calicut had, at one time, been a major port for the export of spices, cloves might have been imported from somewhere and merely re-exported from there.

Then we learnt of an old document which confirmed that the cultivation of cloves in India was first attempted in 1794 when the British asked the governor of Fort St George in Madras to personally ensure the success of a clove plantation. The governor was Lord Hobart and he, eventually, gave his name to the capital of the British colony of Tasmania. Hobart wasn't very successful in his clove project, at first, even though the British had imported strong seedlings from the Moluccas. But their dogged persistence did, finally, pay off and, thanks largely to the efforts of the District Collector of Tirunelvely, E. B. Thomas, the plantation thrived.

A few years earlier, the attempted Dutch stranglehold on cloves had been broken by a wily Frenchman, Pierre Poivre. He had been told that he would become the governor of Ile de France, now known as Mauritius. In 1770 he had some clove seedlings smuggled out of the Moluccas and planted in Mauritius. From there they spread to Zanzibar and Pemba, now in Tanzania. With the British and the French having successfully established clove plantations in their possessions the Dutch were no longer masters of the spice. Once again, spices had changed the economic geography of the world, with people from the cold and temperate lands hurrying to exploit the riches of the warm, tropical, countries.

A panoramic view of the mountain ranges and the plantations and homesteads dotting the valley in Mauritius

C L O V E S

Dried Clove buds look like nails with dark brown stalks and light brown heads

Facing page: A Clove tree showing its height (left); Cloves are the buds of the Clove flower (right above); Dried Cloves (right below)

Clove is a tropical spice. The clove tree needs a well-drained, humus-rich, terrain with a fairly high annual rainfall. It grows to a height of about ten to thirteen metres and starts producing its flowers when it's about six years old. These flowers must not be allowed to produce fruit, not even to open. They have to be plucked, very carefully, when they are still buds, as the appearance of cloves indicate. The buds are dried for several days till their stems have turned dark brown and their heads appreciably lighter. They are now ready to be cleaned, graded, and marketed. They look like little nails which is why they have been called 'cloves' from the French word *clou* meaning nail.

In our family, following an old Anglo-Indian tradition, these 'little nails' are an essential part of Christmas fare most visibly in the traditional Christmas ham. In the past when we had more servants, and much more time, we bought the raw ham and cured it ourselves. Every family had its own curing secrets involving wine, beer, special vegetables, spices and, in our case, boiling over a fragrant wood fire so that the tang of the smoke touched the ham. Then it was allowed to cool, the skin was removed, it was placed on a platter with the cushion side up, a paper frill was tied around the knuckle, breadcrumbs dusted over it and, very carefully, cloves were studded, liberally, into the cushion.

CLOVES

Once, according to a family tale, Grandma was asked, "Why cloves?"

She had looked at her grand-nephew with her perceptive grey eyes. "Because, ham is so rich that it needs something to moderate its effects. Cloves calm the mind, pace the heart, still the digestion and cool the blood. That is why so many Indonesians are a happy people; they even mix cloves in their cigarettes to breathe in its soothing fumes. And because it crackles when it is smoked they call these cigarettes *kretek*."

The cigarette bit is correct. As for the rest, no one had the courage to contradict her.

We're not sure whether cloves really *cool the blood*. Travelling in the Banni, scrublands of Gujarat, we visited a village of horse-breeders who call themselves the Haleputras. They claim to have migrated from Afghanistan countless generations ago but have retained many of their traditions. One of them is the custom for both the bride and groom to wear nuptial masks called *Akhiyo*. They are made of beads and spices. Interestingly, the spices used are cloves possibly for their fragrance, probably to breach barriers of reticence.

We did not have the time in the Haleputra village to find out how the *Akhiyo* had been netted together, but we do know how Grandma made her pomanders to keep her clothes spicily perfumed in an age when women wore forbidding layers of protective garments. The base is a citrus fruit: oranges, lemons, limes even, possibly, *kinnus* those delicious hybrids. Also, fairly large cloves. According to her recipe, the fruit has to be washed and then wiped dry. Then, with a skewer, holes have to be made in the skin of the fruit and cloves liberally inserted in them so that the

pomanders look like fairly bristly pin-cushions. Though Granny didn't mention this, we have found that there is a slight danger of the skin splitting if you make your insertions in a straight line. After the cloves had been inserted into the citrus fruit, Granny would put cinnamon powder in a cloth bag along with the clove-studded citrus fruit and shake the bag well so that the powder was evenly distributed on the pomander balls. She would than arrange the balls on the lid of a cooking pan, though we use a foil tray, and allow them to dry but not in direct sunlight as

Cleaning and drying Cloves

Facing page: In Gujarat's Hodka, descendants of an Afghan tribe retain their Clove-studded bridegroom's masks

CLOVES

that might cause the citrus fruit to sweat. The drying should take about a month as the fruit shrink slowly and harden. Finally, the pomander balls should be put into net bags and either hung in wardrobes or placed in a drawer to diffuse their attractive, and effective, fragrance slowly. A friend assures us that she once used *garam masala* to dust the pomander balls, when she couldn't get unmixed cinnamon powder. Her husband, understandably, was very fond of curries, particularly those tongue searing ones made by the famed Andhra 'Military Hotels'!

Incidentally, we've often wondered why our fairly benign mixture of cinnamon, cardamom and cloves is called *garam masala:* literally the Hot Spice Mix. It doesn't contain chillies or any of its incandescent relatives. The pungent principle in those is capsaicin. But none of these three traditional spices contain any capsaicin. Can the *garam* refer to any other quality in the mixture? Or is that too contentious a claim to consider?

Which brings us to the three root spices which give Indian cuisine much of their distinctiveness. It's difficult to think of our food without them. Having said that, we must admit that India's enormous variety of spices matches its great diversity of people. So though the three root spices are essential to our Anglo-Indian cuisine, and that of very many other communities, we have to admit that they are absolutely anathema to those who view them as dangerously stimulating additions to their food. In fact, the most assertive one is said to possess distinctly psychic powers.

Psychic Guardian

GARLIC

GARLIC

The Devil detests it.

So do Vampires, Werewolves, Witches, Warlocks and all the other 'ghoulies and ghosties' that our worst nightmares can conjure up. Ancient beliefs give good reasons for this. According to an Islamic legend, when the Devil was thrown out of the Garden of Eden, along with our erring First Parents, the first step of his left foot made this spice sprout. Presumably, that cursed foot also carried some of the soil of Paradise. Another, Indic, tale says that just before an Asura could swallow the immortal elixir of the gods that evil impersonator was discovered and the immortality-granting *amrit* fell from his mouth mixed with the saliva of the Asura. Where this liquid was absorbed by the earth, the spice was born. Both beliefs account for the ambivalent qualities of garlic.

Its strong odour tends to repel, but it also contains an antibiotic, *alium:* an antiseptic, expectorant and intestinal antispasmodic to mention just a few of its widely accepted qualities. Traditional wisdom attributes very many more. Our family's very carnivorous diet had been designed for cold, northern, lands where the sun did not appear for many months in the winter. When they migrated to India their strongly non-veg cuisine would have sent them to their graves at an early age. To compensate for their dangerous love of high-protein meals they decided to add four cloves of raw garlic to their breakfast eggs. This, according to a family proverb is because:

'Four cloves a day keep apoplexy at bay'

The many Indian spices sold in South-East Asia include the flavoursome and beneficial Garlic

Facing page: In Malaysia's Johorbahru, descendants of Indian settlers have a thriving spice business

GARLIC

The 'cloves' do not refer to the buds of the *Syzygium aromaticum* but to the egg-shaped bulblets that form the composite garlic bulb. As for *apoplexy*, our venerable Nuttall Dictionary, published in 1929 says:

'Apoplexy n. a sudden deprivation of sense and voluntary motion occasioned by some enforced suspension of the functions of the cerebrum.'

In other words a stroke, possibly caused by High Blood Pressure. Since most of our ancestors lived well into their eighties, longevity genes may not be the only reason, garlic could also be the answer. It is also a fact that the, greatly-praised, 'Mediterranean Diet' is strong on garlic, which could account for their people's unusually low incidence of strokes in spite of their rich diet. In fact the British often made it a point to 'turn up their noses' at the French, Italian, Spanish and Portuguese, claiming that they smelt of garlic. This prejudice, however, began to change as we discovered when we visited the English Isle of Wight.

Wight has the reputation of being the sunniest part of Britain which is, probably, why Queen Victoria and her husband Prince Albert made their getaway palace on the Isle. Albert designed Osborne

House and it was here that her Germanic consort introduced the Brits, and then the British Empire, to the Teutonic practice of the Christmas Tree. But that is another story which we'll tell at some other time.

We were driving to Osborne House down a beautiful wooded road, when we saw the banner. Stretched across our path it proclaimed:

The Garlic Festival
Newchurch IW
August 21/22

A shopper hurries into the Garlic Farm in England's Isle of Wright.

Queen Victoria's stately holiday home, Osborne House, with its many Indian associations, serves only 'English Food' – including *Chicken Tikka Masala*

A Garlic Festival in Britain? But didn't the Brits detest garlic? Or were we witnessing a revolution? Later, in the very, very pucca restaurant in Osborne House, run by the very, very British Heritage Society, they had assured us that they never served pasta—*'That's Italian!'*—and as for crepes suzette, perish the thought—*'It's French! We serve only English food here!'* Amazed, we pointed to *Chicken Tikka Masala* listed on the menu. We were informed, rather coldly, that CTM has been English for very many years. That was, certainly, a gastronomic revolution: the Empire had struck back!

With that experience burbling gleefully in our minds, we headed for the Garlic Farm.

It was really the Mersley Farm and the Garlic Farm Shop was in a beautiful old, thatched, stone cottage set in one of those picture-postcard English gardens: neatly, deliberately, wild and colourful. A peacock and a peahen cast beady eyes on us as Non-Resident Indians sometimes do. Behind them a board announced:

New **GARLIC Ice Cream**—*tastes great*

GARLIC

We decided that anyone who dares to make garlic ice-cream must be very courageous and well worth talking to.

The shop was bright and cheerful and so was the girl behind the counter. There were pods of garlic in willow baskets and metal stands. There were *Oak Smoked Garlic Bulbs*, a basket of *Elephant Garlic* and a whole range of garlic relishes including three new ones:

Vampire's Revenge
Plum Garlic and Habenero Chilli, try with ice-cream?

Cheeky Monkey
Garlic and Banana great with Thai and Indian

Daredevil (very hot)
With pineapple, garlic and chilli mustard.

According to the creative farmer, Colin Boswell, many rich British tourists spend their holidays in the Mediterranean. Very adroitly, Boswell positioned garlic as the way to rediscover the mood, to recapture memories of moonlit nights and romance by evoking the warm flavour of garlic, when they return from their sunny

Britons, returning from Mediterranean holidays, associated the taste of Garlic with the warmth of sun-drenched vacations. The Garlic Farm's wide range of products taps into this nostalgia

Med holiday to their Nine-to-Five lives under the grey skies of Britain. This very innovative entrepreneur had turned a seeming disadvantage, the smell of garlic, into its unique marketing proposition: *The Smell of Affluence!*

When we spoke to him, Boswell's farm covered twenty-five acres, employed two hundred people and grew eight different kinds of garlic. Clearly, Wight has the sunshine and the fertile, sandy, loamy soil that the spice prefers. "Garlic is a cultivar," Boswell said. "If you choose the largest bulbs for planting, your crop will continue to improve."

Other garlic farmers could also enhance their fortunes by thinking out of the box, the way Boswell did. Folklore, for instance, is a major source of inherited wisdom in all Asian countries. We believe that all Indic beliefs, however mythical their origins

Garlic has a long shelf life and is ever-present in most Indian kitchens

might sound, conceal cores of scientific truths passed down from generation to generation in easily remembered tales. How then, we asked ourselves, did a spice which had such menacing origins as the saliva of a demon, come to be regarded as a virtual cure-all? One reason could be that a little bit of a noxious substance can cause the body to build up its own defences against more aggressive attacks. Homeopathy works on this principle. So too, for that matter, does the allopathic system of vaccines. Does garlic fortify the immune system of the body? Possibly, and ancient civilisations appear to have known about its defensive properties.

As we have described in our first chapter, *A Prevalence of Spices*, the armies of labourers who toiled in the blistering heat of Egypt to build the great pyramids, were given liberal rations of raw garlic to keep them fit. Roman legions, we learn, were also garlic eaters because, they believed, it gave them courage. In all probability it warded off the many debilitating infections that the wandering soldiers would have been exposed to in their world-conquering campaigns.

This habit seems to have been handed down to all the Latin races influenced

Garlic pods produce
the health capsules
called garlic cloves

"

GARLIC

by the Romans. The other, paler, races of Europe call them 'hot blooded' and say that they have over-active hormones. This back-handed admiration of the libido-enhancing effects of unclogged arteries, brought about by a diet rich in garlic, finds endorsement in our lore. Traditionally, widows are not expected to eat garlic because it would 'warm' their blood. In fact, in many traditional societies, widows were often accused of bringing about the death of their husbands by attracting malign influences. Since their families also believed in the cure-all properties of garlic, by depriving them of this spice which, in effect, was a broad-spectrum anti-biotic fighting against infections brought about by invading protozoa, parasites, viruses and fungi, they virtually ensured the early demise of these unfortunate women. Inspiration can, however, be drawn from this deliberately neglectful practice. If research can establish such wide-ranging beneficial effects of garlic, a whole new market for the spice would be opened up. It would be much larger than the innovative *Smell of Affluence* strategy of Colin Boswell of the Isle of Wight.

But, as we have discovered, the protective power of garlic goes far beyond shielding humans from malign powers and illnesses.

In our small Himalayan cottage, our parents had planted a few high-yielding peach trees. For many years they sprayed those trees with Bordeaux Mixture to ward off the crippling leaf-curl disease. One year, however, our family was away from our cottage during the crucial early Spring period. When we returned, it was too late to spray the trees and so, sadly, we reconciled ourselves to a season of afflicted trees and withered peaches. To our surprise, however, the trees and their leaves thrived and we had a great crop of juicy fruit. We had no explanation till, one day, a soft-spoken farmer from our Garhwal Hills visited us. We told him what had happened and he nodded his head and said he'd like to see our trees. We walked to the upper garden with him and stood near the peach trees. He pointed down and said, "There is your doctor!" At the base of the trees, because cultivable land is scarce in the mountains, we had grown small beds of garlic. "I don't

Fresh Garlic uprooted from the soil, with tuber and stalk

Facing page: Garlic plants absorbing strength from the sun (above); Field of Garlic plant (below)

GARLIC

know why it happens" he said, "but I have noticed that when I grow garlic near my peach trees, they never get leaf curl." Do garlic bulbs spread their defensive properties through the soil? If they do, geneticists might like to develop strains of garlic tailored to defend specific cash crops from their microbial predators.

Bulbs, corms, tubers and the other root-storage systems developed by plants contain all that the plant needs to start it on its journey through life. These storehouses of goodness must have been discovered by our ancestors many generations ago.

They even found one that gave them so much zest that it became a synonym for hyperactivity and excitement.

The Rhizome of Zest

GINGER

GINGER

Winter is ginger time.

When the stars twinkle icicle-bright in our high Himalayan sky, and the wild-geese fly back from the chill Tibetan lakes, honking in the moonlit sky, it is time to break out our very special golden wine. We call it a 'wine' but it isn't alcoholic. It's been brewed according to an old, and very secret, recipe created by some remote, but unknown, ancestor.

It's a Ginger Wine, a celebration of a spice that is the epitome of zest.

When we first tasted it, as children, we were thrilled. It had the tingle that we had associated with surreptitious, and totally forbidden, sips of Christmas punch. But … and this was the wondrous thing about it … we were permitted to have our own little glasses of it making us feel very grown up and superior. We now learn that the bite of ginger lies in its essential oils and oleo-resins which have all sorts of curative powers built into them, according to ancient Indian traditions. We believe that ginger is, essentially, an Indian spice and that it was carried by our traders all across the world: even though some Caucasian 'experts' claim that it was first 'discovered' by the Chinese.

For one thing, ginger is a very hungry, tropical, crop. It demands warmth and moisture, bright sunshine, heavy rain and a rich, sandy loam. It is so voracious that it exhausts the soil and a ginger crop cannot be followed by another ginger crop unless the soil has been renewed

Freshly cut slices of Ginger

Right: A field of Ginger

GINGER

either by nature, or by growing something else on it in between. Drenching annual rains, in Kerala, bringing down rich humus from wooded mountains and spreading it across the lowlands, are nature's way of replenishing the earth with the nutrients that ginger needs. Ginger's rhizomes then suck up this natural goodness, convert it by an efficient bio-chemical process, and store it so that the ginger plant can produce its lush crop of leaves about a metre in height. These leaves, by the magic of photosynthesis which uses sunlight as an energy source, add to the life-giving qualities stored in the rhizomes.

We have, deliberately, romanticised the role of the leaves of the ginger plant even though all leaves are solar-powered chemical factories. But it is in ginger, in particular, that the tongue and the palate can, virtually, taste the sharp goodness of sunlight locked in the essential oils of this remarkable spice.

The great Ayurvedic masters of our land realised that cures, like justice, must not only be effective but they must also feel to be efficacious. They gave ginger two titles: *Mahabheshaj,* the Universal Doctor, and *Mahaoushdhi,* the Greatest Medicine. They prescribed it for many things from obesity and skin diseases, indigestion, loss of appetite and tumours, through a wide range of fevers, to easing thirst, stopping shivering and even improving the quality of breast milk. As for the non-vegetarians of our land: ginger-garlic paste is an essential ingredient in virtually all meat dishes because it helps to digest proteins.

Clearly the fame of this spicy panacea was carried by Indian traders to China. The evolution of its name gives away its provenance. The Chinese call ginger *Chiang.* This seems to have been derived from the Sanskrit *Singabera* or 'horn shaped.' Our Sanskrit name also influenced ginger's Latin designation for the spice: *Zingiber officinale.* In fact most of the other variations of the name, in many languages of the world, reflect the Indian origin of the word including the English *Ginger.*

The English have had a long-standing affair with ginger. Long before Henry of

Left: In Sarawak, Borneo, Indian spices including Ginger are in great demand. Sarawak was once ruled by the descendants of an East India Company trader and were known as the White Rajas

Right: Fresh Ginger

A pounding stone creates chutney from spices or, as the French would say, a *roche carri* to make *chatini*

GINGER

Normandy brought his troops across the English Channel, and conquered the ill-prepared people in the Misty Isles, ginger had been greatly valued. A pound of ginger cost as much as a sheep. One reason for the popularity of ginger in the colder parts of the world is that ginger is an effective pain killer and it also reduces inflammation and keeps cold-aggravated ailments, like arthritic pains and aching joints, at bay. Consequently, ginger had a long time to work its friendly way into the English vocabulary while still retaining its vitality and effervescence, much like the popular ginger beer.

A *Ginger Group* is a small group of people whose object is to stir the more passive into activity. Our 21st century social media seem to offer fertile ground for the growth of such fizzy, hyper-active, cults. Such agitations, however, are not a new phenomena. The 16th century English king, Henry VIII, was so gingered up that he went through six wives, helping some to lose their heads, protested against the anti-divorce views of the church, and even got his nobles to write letters in support of his 'liberal' stand. These letters were tied in red tape and so they gave the world a new term for officialese! But that's just an interesting little aside to the ginger tale.

Henry VIII's powerful daughter, Queen Elizabeth I, and her court, chomped on gingerbread. It wasn't bread but a biscuit with a sharp, gingery, flavour and its popularity filtered down to the common man. That great recorder of his tumultuous times, William Shakespeare, in his *Twelfth Night*, has the clown say:

'… *and ginger shall be hot i' the mouth too*.'

The zing … a word for energy or excitement … of *Zingiber*, had become so necessary to Europeans, to relieve the blandness of their diet, that a whole street in Basle was called the Imbergasse, the 'Ginger Alley.' As happened with pepper, traders got fed up with the monopolistic arm-twisting of Arab middlemen. The 16th century saw large-scale plantings of ginger in the West Indies where the environmental conditions were similar to those of Kerala and other monsoon lands.

The Arabs were so convinced of the ambrosial qualities of ginger that they found it easy to accept the view expressed in the Koran. That great spiritual book, revealed to the Prophet Mohammed, says that those righteous souls who ascend to Paradise refresh themselves by sharing libations of a festive drink of which ginger is a significant ingredient.

The English could have picked up echoes of this teaching during their encounters with the great Islamic civilisation in the Crusades. It took a while percolating into their insular mindset but after the English East India Company had opened the mores and tastes of the British, their inn-keepers were forced to add a certain tropical animation to their fermented beverages. They left bowls of dried ginger powder for their beer-quaffing customers and encouraged them to sprinkle it on their drinks and then stir it in with a red-hot poker possibly, but not always, with a little sugar. This was, clearly, an adaptation of the mulled wine technique to a mulled beer or ale. We see the influence of ayurveda in this. According to our Indic physicians, ginger cures enlargement of the spleen and liver. So, presumably, if you added ginger to your tipple you countered the effects of drinking not wisely but too well.

This could also have been the reason behind the old tradition, in our family, of nibbling on candied, preserved and crystallised ginger in winter. During these cold months, social drinking increases. In anticipation of this, we would buy fair quantities of succulent green ginger. These rhizomes were peeled very carefully, cut into nibble-sized chunks, and then boiled. After which they were soaked in a sugar solution. When they emerged from this treatment they were brown and frosted with crystals of sugar. These were then packed into antique, ceramic, Chinese ginger jars. Then, when the nights got a chill bite in them generally, when chevrons of wild geese and ducks flew over the Himalayas and into their wintering wetlands in our

Dried Ginger preserves the virtue of the rhizomes

Fat, fleshy rhizomes of
fresh Ginger

plains, the first ginger jar was opened. In spite of the fat rhizomes having been boiled, the fragrant, wake-up, aroma of ginger was mouth-watering. And every bite filled the mouth with the radiance of sunshine.

It doesn't make a whit of difference to us when chemists assert that the scent of ginger lies in its essential oils, used to give an aura of energy to men's after-shave lotions. They also claim that the flavour of ginger resides with its oleo-resins which go into the English ginger beer and the American ginger ale. When we savoured our crystallised ginger, the blended essential oil and oleo-resins combined to capture the warm, wild, ambiance of summer.

Sadly, very sadly, when we moved back to our home in the oak woods of the Himalayas, the Chinese ginger jars were misplaced as was an old recipe book with yellowing pages and faded copper-plate writing. We've forgotten the critical techniques of making preserved/ crystallised/candied ginger.

We did, however, have a little success in another field. During the years we were

Half dried Ginger

GINGER

in Kerala, we learnt how to grow our own ginger. A planter friend taught us how to cultivate it, when to harvest it and how to dry it. He then showed us how to distinguish it from its look-alike relative which we also grew in our garden. From the lush, southern, palm-whispering, polder-lands of Kerala we returned to the oak woods of the great northern mountains. We now live 2,000 metres high in the Himalayas. Yesterday, when we went for a walk in the saffron-dusted dusk, we were surprised to find that our neighbour was growing that closely related spice in a small patch of hillside.

Next year, with a little bit of luck, we'll grow that other member of the *Zingiberacea* family in our own Himalayan garden. Their rhizomes also form an important ingredient in our cuisine. And, from our personal experience, they are even more therapeutic.

Left: A Ginger plant

Right: The Chinese snacked on Ginger preserve stored in special ceramic jars

The Golden Healer

TURMERIC

They're the peacocks of our high mountains.

The long tailed magpies are plumed in blue and trail two, long, feathers behind them. They spend their summers in the higher Himalayas and when they arrive, in families of six to eight, we know that winter is around the corner. One winter, tragedy struck. There was the *crack!* of a shot and the trigger-happy sons of a transient neighbour felled one of these beautiful, graceful, birds. We read the riot act to the fiends and then, with great difficulty, our son rescued the bird from the ravine where it was cowering in terror. We didn't think it would live, but Mum gave it a tot of her rare Napoleon brandy and bound its damaged wing with a poultice and splint. We kept him in a covered cage near our log fire. "If it has to die," Mum said, "let it die in warmth and comfort."

To our delight, it did not die. In fact, the next morning it squawked, asking for food. We named him Dickey. He lived for many years, formed a sentry partnership with Honey, our brilliant Apso Terrier and, amazingly, repeatedly sounded the alarm whenever a stranger entered our grounds. He could distinguish between one of our staff and an outsider. So much for being 'bird-brained'. Dickey never recovered his full powers of flight but he did manage to flap up to his perch in his day aviary, wish

Peacock, India's national bird

Right: The north face of Mount Everest as seen from the path to the base camp in Tibet

TURMERIC

goodbye to his flock when summer came, and greet them when they returned in winter.

The miraculous poultice that Mum had used to knit the shattered bones of Dickey's wing was a paste of golden-yellow, turmeric. She had learnt about its healing powers from our Santhal gardener in Bihar. His father, he told us, had been a famed folk-healer: an *Ojha*.

Western science has not, apparently, accepted the curative properties of *Curcuma longa*. They view it only as a condiment used to make 'curry powder' and the ingredient that gives a rich colour

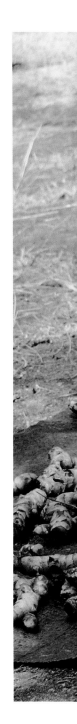

to dishes from many parts of our land. The orange-yellow tint is attributed to curcumin but we have not been able to find any authoritative western writer willing to credit any therapeutic qualities to either curcumin or turmeric.

This is curious, to say the least. Particularly when virtually all authorities admit that turmeric is widely used in Asian, and particularly South-Asian, cuisine. The Vedas, the greatly revered spiritual and social scriptures of the Aryan people, recommended it for the treatment of jaundice and leprosy. Both diseases show their effects on the skin of the sufferers and in other ways, too. Turmeric is widely used in Asia as a skin lotion. Some foreign writers believe that Asian women prefer the yellow glow that turmeric water imparts to their skin to the pink that Occidental females opt for. We found this reasoning to be far-fetched particularly when we learnt that, in Malaysia, turmeric paste is applied to the abdomens of women after they have given birth, and to the cut umbilical cord of their babies, to speed up the healing process. Here, in our land, we are assured that many women use turmeric paste on their faces to improve the tone of their skin and to prevent the growth of facial hair. There is

Fresh Turmeric laid out to dry

Left: Spices of fresh Turmeric rhizomes: showing the inner texture

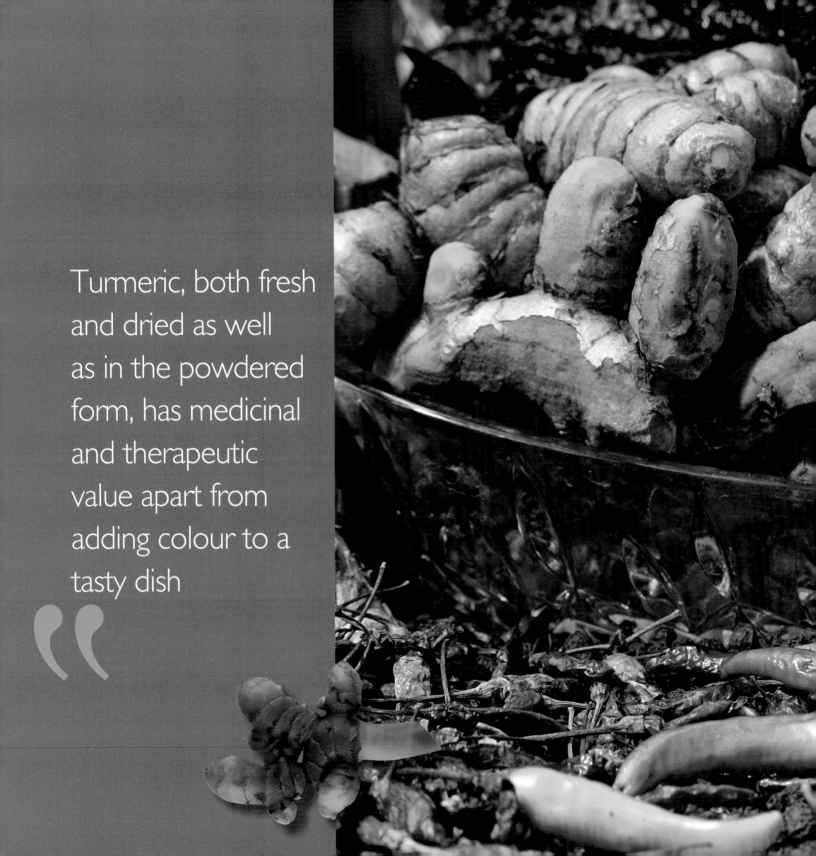

Turmeric, both fresh and dried as well as in the powdered form, has medicinal and therapeutic value apart from adding colour to a tasty dish

"

TURMERIC

also a strong Asian belief that turmeric taken as a medicine, cures stomach aches, 'cools fevers' to quote a Malayali friend, and is excellent for the prevention of stomach ulcers and liver ailments. Since he comes from a long line of hard-drinking, long-living, planters we treat his opinion with great respect!

Then we came across an excellent article in *Indian Spices* written by nutritionist Ruth N. Davidar: 'Cooking With Spices is Healthy'. She says:

> "Turmeric has recently been found to reduce the risk of cancer and heart disease because of two substances, namely curcumin and turmeric (which seems to be a misprint for *tumerone*), both of which are powerful antioxidants. Antioxidants help to arrest the damaging effects of waste products generated as a result of cell metabolism, or from external factors such as car exhaust and tobacco smoke. Turmeric also has anti-inflammatory properties and can lower blood cholesterol. … As is readily evident, spices do not merely flavour and preserve food in a hot, tropical climate like ours as was previously thought."

Spices also have a significant nutritional and therapeutic value.

This brought us back to our planter friend from Kerala. He told us that we should harvest our crop of turmeric only when the leaves start yellowing. Then, according to him, turmeric farmers lift the rhizomes, carefully, wash them, remove the roots and put the trimmed turmeric in a metal pot with enough water to cover the rhizomes. The empty space in the pot is then stuffed with turmeric leaves after which the mouth is covered with gunny sacking and sealed with mud. The pot is now placed over a slow fire, allowed to boil for about three hours, and then cooled. The boiled rhizomes are removed, spread out, and

A field of Turmeric

Washed Turmeric
ready for boiling

Above: Women
washing freshly
harvested Turmeric

Basketfuls of Fresh Turmeric. In India, fresh turmeric is used in traditional medicine, home remedies and as an organic, natural cosmetic in beauty applications

TURMERIC

dried in the sun for about a week. This, however, is not the end of the process. The dried turmeric rhizomes have to be polished either by rubbing them in an abrasive pottery device or by rotating them in a metal cylinder. All this is, clearly, very labour intensive.

It seems unlikely that turmeric farmers would take such pains to prepare turmeric for the market if all that the spice did was to colour the food and give it a faint flavour, as western writers would have us believe. In spite of the soaring popularity of Indian food, Caucasian researchers seem to have deliberately ignored, or consistently downplayed, our traditional wisdom about the therapeutic virtues of turmeric. It could be a variation of colour-prejudice. Not a racial colour bias but a culinary one. Turmeric is associated with the colour of Asian food which was, till the post-colonial Asian Diaspora, shunned by Europeans. It was considered to be a sub-standard cuisine not worthy of the attention of sophisticated gourmets and chefs. Even today, no ingredient used in western cooking has the vivid, long-lasting, colour of food cooked with turmeric. This, possibly, upsets the fastidious sensibilities of those who consider frogs and snails as gourmet fare. Contrary to skewed Occidental 'wisdom', it is clear that the vivid, pervasive, colour of turmeric is one of its plus points. It is a strong chromatic indicator.

Left: Freshly harvested Turmeric with mud sticking to the roots and on the rhizomes

Raw Turmeric rhizomes have a golden glow after being washed

Drying of boiled
Turmeric: this is a
week-long process

Above: Boiling of
the fresh rhizomes

Turmeric is also marketed as powder and in encapsulated form

"

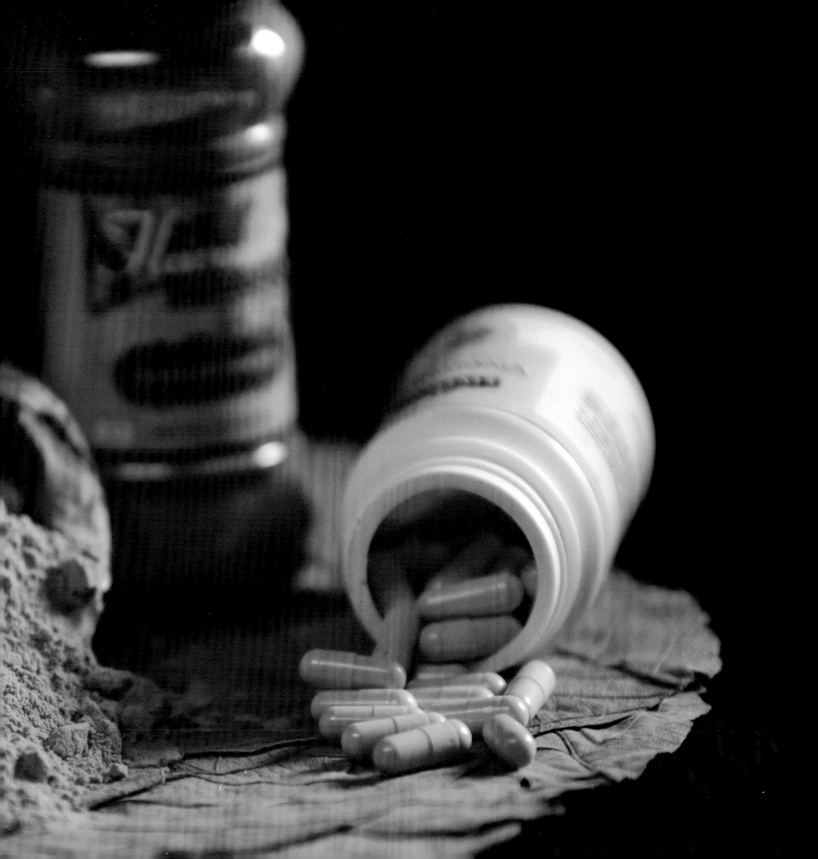

TURMERIC

We believe that turmeric serves the same purpose in Asian cuisine as pepper did in European food in the pre-refrigeration days. In the cosseting heat and humidity of our tropical lands, fresh ingredients don't stay fresh for long. They are attacked by microbial predators. The addition of turmeric to the food repels quick-breeding biological invaders and maintains its taste and nutritional values. The tell-tale golden-orange colour of turmeric is, consequently, an assurance that the food is still fit to eat because, if turmeric is not stored carefully and sealed even against something even so innocuous as light, its colour changes. If it is still golden-orange, it is still effective.

Not only should our food scientists bring the many virtues of turmeric to the attention of the world, but Indian gourmets should also assert themselves. It's about time that the foodies of India instituted their own version of the French *Cordon bleu*. A suitable designation could be *Cordon d'or;* The Golden Ribbon, for Sub-continental cookery of the highest quality, and to recognise the all-pervasive role of golden turmeric.

Which brings us to the spice most vociferously, and most erroneously, associated with Indian food. Some people would have us believe that this family of strong-tasting herbs was brought to Asia from the Americas after Christopher Columbus lost his way while searching for India. Thanks to another accidental discovery, by a former colleague, it is clear to us that this superbly pungent spice is as Indian as curry..

Turmeric powder. A feast for the eye

Left: Turmeric in encapsulated form

Fiery Controversy

CHILLIES

We are about to commit a spicy sacrilege.

We intend to contradict some of the sacred scriptures of spices. According to Frederic Rosengarten Jr's *The Book of Spices:*

"Paprika, red pepper, and cayenne pepper are ground condiments made from the juiceless ripe, dried pods of plants of the genus *Capsicum,* commonly known as chilli peppers or chillies. They are members of the *Solanaceae* (nightshade family) indigenous to Mexico, Central America, the West Indies, and much of South America."

Very clearly, according to this authority, this whole family of spices belongs to the Americas. With equally assertive authority, both John W. Parry and the venerated *Encyclopaedia Britannica* share the same view.

We don't.

We differ because of an experience we had some years ago when one of us, in an earlier professional incarnation, was an officer in the Indian Navy. That year our ship was on patrol around our Andaman archipelago. These little wooded islands are largely uninhabited except for scattered communities of indigenes like the Jarawas. There are some anthropologists who believe that these Negrito people were the first inhabitants of our land paddling in from Africa when the oceans were shallower than they are now because the Ice Age had frozen much of the water. Other scientists, very tentatively, contend that an independent stream of *Homo sapiens* originated in India and the Jarawas

Luscious hot Chillies
ripe for plucking

are descendants of the first humans in the sub-continent to evolve into *Thinking Man*. If they did evolve here then, obviously, they didn't paddle in from anywhere.

The important point, however, is that neither theory claims that they came from the Americas or the West Indies.

So when one of our colleagues brought back a bunch of tiny chillies from a remote Andaman Island, those little spices must have been indigenous to that place. In the wardroom at lunch in *INS Rajput,* that afternoon, we bit into them. They were so hot that they nearly burnt our scalps off! Sweat streamed off us and we gulped water and chilled beer to cool ourselves.

This fierce reaction captured our imaginations and we started to read up all we could about this spice.

Fresh red Chillies

We discovered that the great family *Solanaceae* has an almost human ability to adapt itself to varying climates, terrains, soil and climatic conditions. It also responds, very flexibly, to cultivation and selection by farmers. Thus, this pungent spice was gentled by Hungarian cultivators into the mild *paprika* and added to their 'herdsmen's meat' stew, *goulash.* In Spain, however, the size of the original chillies increased, they lost much of their pungent, crystalline, capsaicin, and became the capsicum we recognise in India today. This variant does not take kindly to a warm climate which is why it is often referred to as *Shimla Mirch,* the Chilli of Shimla, in North India. The Americans, and some of our modern Indian TV chefs, refer to them as 'bell peppers' because of their shape. Back in 1753, Swedish botanist, Carolus Linnaeus described two species of capsicum, but only fourteen years later he had identified two more. A century later, Botanist A. Fingerhuth had raised the count to twenty-five. Though it's difficult to keep up with this adaptable spice, it is generally recognised that there are five cultivated varieties. Leading the popularity vote is *C. annuum* and it has both sweet and pungent pods. 'Bird's eye pepper' is a variant of this. *C. chinense* likes the

In a village
market, a
woman sells
chillies grown in
her homestead ,,

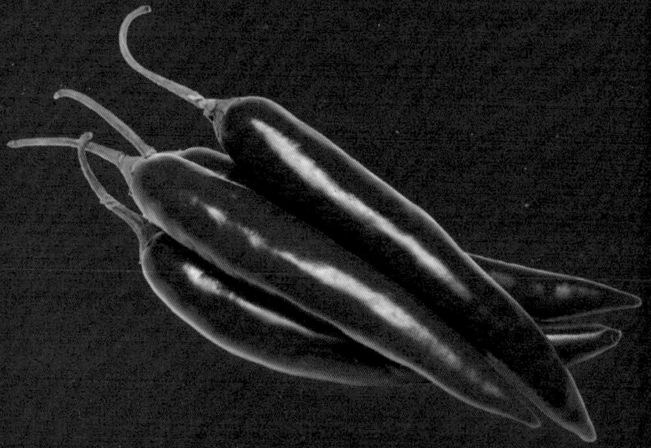

CHILLIES

lowlands and has round and pungent fruit. It spiced a fiery, vindaloo-like dish we relished in Havana. *C. pendulum,* favoured in the Andean states of Ecuador, Peru and Bolivia, has yellow or brown spotted flowers and pungent fruit with a conical shape. It grows at the highest elevations of all chillies. *C. pubescens,* as its name suggests, is a hairy chilli with small, oblong, red and orange pods and black seeds. *C. frutescens* is probably the one responsible for misleading our spice pundits. It's the one that the Spanish conquistadors, plundering South America, hailed as the plant closest to the Indian pepper they were searching for. They also brought back the Nahuatl word, from the people of South and Central America, *chilli.* It originally described a perennial shrub which grows to a height of about two metres, has white flowers with a greenish tinge, and stems which are woodier than those of the other varieties. Its product is the main ingredient in Tabasco sauce, toned down a bit for barbecue sauce. It also helps add an extra zest to the zing in ginger ale and ginger beer.

The use of chillies to enrich these popular western delights might come as a surprise to some Caucasians, even though they are, now, more adventurous in their choice of food and drink.

Dried Chillies are even 'hotter'

Nevertheless, during our trips abroad we often hear the phrase, "I love Indian food, but I can't take too much of it. I find it very pungent." This is largely because the traditional European idea of "Indian Food" is a stew liberally doused with 'Curry Powder': a makeshift, pungent, ingredient that most Indian housewives would shun. We try to reassure our pale friends that most Indian food is not fiery with chillies. The cuisine of Kerala is largely bereft of this spice. Kashmiri cuisine, though often red with the skin of dried chillies, shuns the pungent seed. And in our travels in the Himalayas, from its western extremity to its north-eastern tip, we have found that chillies are not a favoured spice of these highland people. There is a significant exception in one North-eastern state which we shall come to. In general, however, as we explain to our foreign friends, the hotter the climate, the hotter the food. Chillies promote sweating, cooling the body. They also help in digesting starchy foods like rice by enhancing the secretion of gastric juices. But since not all Indians eat starchy foods all the time, and not all of India is hot all year round, not all Indian food needs to be charged with pungent chillies.

We specify *pungent* chillies because not all chillies are pungent. At last count we were

Right: What a sight. Fiery, yes of course

Many Indian spices are grown by small farmers and sold fresh within a few hours of their being harvested, as this man is doing in a traditional weekly *haat*

Women harvesting chillies from a chilly field looking cool and composed.
Inset is the 'hot fruit' of their labour

CHILLIES

told, there were over ninety species of chillies, though perhaps it would be more correct to describe them as varieties, rather than species. A spice farmer assures us, however, that all chilli seeds should be kept for a year before being planted. Against that expert advice is the one we have received from a close relative. In her north-Indian family, when chillies bought for the kitchen get soft and a little short of rotting, the seeds are scattered in a backyard bed. These, otherwise discarded, seeds eventually, give a good crop of chilli

plants even though they have not been kept aside for a year. We take no sides in these seemingly conflicting methods so it might be worthwhile to try both.

Generally speaking, however, chilli seeds are sown so that when the flowering begins, about three months later, the weather should be fairly warm and dry. Flowering lasts for another three months and then, if the weather gods are kind, the farmer should get five or six pickings. Because chilli plants are, apparently, prolific,

The adaptable Chilli comes in various shapes, sizes and pungency

undemanding and adaptable, we see a growth in the consumption of chillies reaching out across the world. Every time a new pizza parlour opens, catering to the burgeoning fast-food craze, the chilli market grows. Italian dishes use a great deal of 'pizza pepper' or 'peperone rosso': crushed red chillies. Cayenne pepper is neither grown in Cayenne, West Africa, nor is it pepper. It is made from ground red chillies. Not only do chillies have the same red colouring matter that is found in carrots, carotene, but they also have an additional virtue. In 1937, Hungarian scientist, Dr. Szent-Gyorgyi, won the Nobel Prize for discovering that paprika pods were one of the greatest sources of Vitamin C, even richer than the better known citrus fruits.

Vitamin C seems to give a strong boost to the immune system, warding off all sorts of microbial predators drifting around us. Perhaps the lean, athletic, fitness of Ethiopian long-distance runners could be attributed, in part at least, to the unique way in which their people use chillies. According to our rare, 150-year old, *Encyclopaedia Asiatica*:

> "The *wort* may be termed the traditional dish of the Abyssinians. Equal parts of salt and red cayenne pods are powdered and mixed together with a little pea or bean meal to make a paste. This is called *dillock* and is made in large quantities at a time being preserved in a large shell generally suspended from the roof. The *wort* is merely a little water added to this paste, which is then boiled over the fire, with the addition of a little fat meat and more meal to make a kind of porridge to which is also added several warm seeds such as the common cress or black mustard both of which are indigenous in Abyssinia."

Sackfuls of red fire.
Ready for the market

CHILLIES

Sounds interesting, particularly as the mountains of Ethiopia can be cold and misty. Capsaicin reputedly shrinks inflamed mucous membranes, easing blocked noses and sinuses, making it easier to take in the long breaths needed by marathon runners.

Just recently we have also learnt of a new, and very stimulating use, of the extract of chillies. According to a report, attributed to *Asia News International,* the 'hotness' of a chilli is measured in Scoville units. *'It denotes how many times the chilli must be diluted by its own mass of water until the heat is only just discernible.'* It goes on to say that an English spirits company has bottled a fiery vodka cocktail: English vodka mixed with the hottest chillies in the world. These chillies have an incredible rating of one million Scovilles, according to the report carried in the *Hindustan Times* of 27 September 2012.

The chillies are the King Chillies which, in an article carried by the authoritative *Spice India* magazine of the Spices Board:

… is thought to originate from Nagaland.

Perhaps the Americas-India controversy about the origin of chillies will be solved by a DNA analysis. All living things have

A fiery carpet of Chillies

DNA which can establish relationships. It is also possible that the chillies of the Americas and those of India are a case of parallel evolution. But till that is done we'll hold on to our belief: Chillies did not originate in the Americas but in India.

Which brings us to another spice seed which also has acknowledged 'hot' properties.

The Spanish Trailblazer

MUSTARD

MUSTARD

The little silver pot intrigued him.

The pale winter sun of the Himalayas lanced in through the skylight, shot highlights off the embossed silver, glowed on the blue glass that lined it, glinted off the tiny spoon with the almond-shaped bowl. He reached out and touched it as if he couldn't believe what he saw. He claimed to be an American folklorist and antiquarian who had heard that our cottage in the oak woods dated back to 1831 and held a number of heirlooms. We had asked him to join us for Christmas lunch.

He said "That's a mustard pot, isn't it?" He didn't wait for our reply before adding.

"This is not my speciality but, if I'm not wrong, they first appeared in the 14th century but there are no extant examples

earlier than the 17th. This one seems to be late Victorian, probably crafted by an Indian silversmith for an English company. The glass could be the famous Bath Blue." He seemed to be talking to himself. Then he snapped out of his soliloquy. "But there's no mustard in it!"

"No, not yet." We explained. "Fifteen minutes before we sit down to dinner, we'll mix mustard powder, salt, sugar and vinegar, stir it till it's well blended, put it aside to 'work'. Then we'll spoon the paste into the mustard pot and it'll be nice and sharp to go with our roast."

He smiled and nodded his head. "Oh right!" He prolonged the *right* till it sounded *raaiiight*. "And that's how you

Above: A red ceramic cruet from Cyprus, with a Mustard Pot; a traditional silver-and-glass one; and a modern pot in a Swedish design. Mustard Pots are distinguished by their small spoons, often inserted through a hole in the aroma-protecting lid.

Right: Himalayas lanced in through the skylight

MUSTARD

still do it!" he nodded again and we could almost see his brain registering it under Anglo-Indian Customs: Mustard Pots for the Christmas Roast. He caught us looking at him and added, hurriedly, "OK! OK! Back home in the states we squeeze it out of a tube. So what's so special about mixing it like you said?"

It was time to get back to our guests in the drawing room, refresh their glasses, recharge the bowls of chips and nuts, so our reply was rather hurried.

"Because mustard powder has no smell and no taste. When we mix it afresh, with water, and let it stand for ten minutes or so, its enzymes produce an oil not found in the plant, giving it its hot, tangy taste. The vinegar then steps in and slows its enzyme activity and its sharp taste stays till we finish the meal. The Romans used fermented grape juice or *mustum* instead of vinegar, so they called the tongue-tingling product *mustum ardens,* hot must. That's how we got the word Mustard."

He seemed a little embarrassed and said, "Is that right?" In American usage it's as much an explanation as a question and requires no answer. Then a thought struck him and he grinned. "Don't tell me that

Close-up of a Mustard field in bloom

Facing page:
Mustard field spreading a bright yellow carpet for the eye to feast on

all those acres and acres of yellow fields we passed in Rajasthan grow mustard for little pots like these?" He was right about Rajasthan, wrong about the use of mustard in our land. According to a news-report Rajasthan accounts for 54 per cent of our country's mustard production.

We shepherded him back into the party and so we did not tell him that very few Indians used table mustard and that the majority of the mustard fields he had seen would go into producing mustard oil and mustard greens, *sarsoo ka saag.* Americans seem to believe that mustard is best used as a paste to flavour hot dogs and fast foods. Most Caucasians have lost whatever little knowledge their ancestors had about the medicinal and fortifying virtues of the mustard plant.

But our people haven't. The sharp, almost resinous, aroma of mustard oil brings back visions of eastern India: of Bengal's delectable Mustard Fish eaten on a river vessel moving slowly down the rippled currents of the Hooghly. And there are earlier memories. In Bihar, where one of us was born, mustard oil was believed to be a sure defence against coughs, colds and 'flu. Whenever we were exposed to damp and cold weather, our throats,

MUSTARD

chests, backs and the soles of our feet were rubbed down with hot mustard oil. It soothed and warmed us and we soon fell into a deep, refreshing, sleep. It did make one smell a bit like a *pakora* … we called them *philaurees* in our variant of kitchen Hinglish … but we never suffered from the sneezes and sore-throats of winter.

In the cold, damp, climes of Western Europe, the therapeutic properties of Mustard prompted various European monarchs, particularly those of France, to consume truly large quantities of mustard paste at their banquets. One was so obsessed by this spice that he carried his own portion of mustard with him whenever he went out to dine. This was a good precaution. In those unhygienic days, mustard tended to retard decomposition brought about by bacteria.

In fact, like most spices, mustard was first valued for its therapeutic qualities. A mustard plaster, made by sandwiching a layer of mustard paste between two pieces of cloth was a home remedy for aches, pains and swellings of the joints and muscles. A Santhal herbal doctor in Bihar said that *'its heat draws out the pain.'* A Registered Medical Practitioner, who was a shade above a modern para-medic, said

that the mustard causes a mild irritation to the skin, giving the impression of warmth, and makes blood rush to the spot. This increased circulation induces greater activity by the defensive white blood cells and creates antibodies which, in turn, remove the effects of the infection or trauma. Both could be spouting their own versions of gobbledegook but the bottom line is that the mustard plaster worked every time.

Or, perhaps, we should say that the medicinal properties of our black, tropical, mustard worked every time. *Brassica nigra* of our tropics, grows a shade taller than *Brassica hirta* of the temperate lands. Both have yellow flowers and their striking colour was used as a botanical guide by

A Mustard flower in close-up. Lower down one can see the pods containing the harmless looking hot seeds

Facing page:
Harvested Mustard seeds

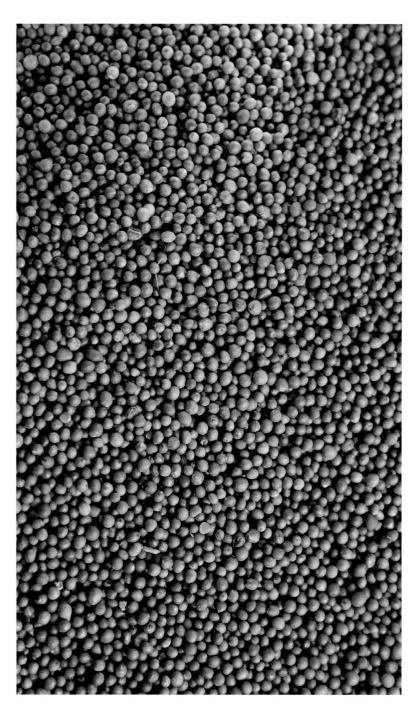

the Spanish monks when they landed in America. Trudging along the west coast of what was to become the USA, they scattered mustard seeds as markers of the route they had taken. To this day, the yellow flowers of wild mustard mark the old mission stations named after saints of the Catholic church: Santa Barbara, San Diego and San Francisco.

Such blazing stretches of golden blooms also appear in our northern states, particularly Rajasthan, Punjab and Haryana. Traditional wisdom ascribes winter-combating properties to mustard leaves, called *sarsoo ka saag,* particularly if eaten with *rotis* made of corn meal with lashings of hot *ghee* technically known as clarified butter. And to add to the richness of this super-sustaining dish, it is accompanied with a lump of jaggery. This is washed down with the yoghurt drink, *lassi.* This is, possibly, where the hyper-energetic *bhangra* dancers get their zest and stamina from!

The *Encyclopaedia Britannica* says:

> Plants raised for leaves are grown in the
> spring or fall because only basal leaves
> from fast-growing plants are suitable in pot
> herbs. Plants raised for seeds are grown in

MUSTARD

summer, when flowering occurs early and few leaves appear'.

Possibly; but according to a report attributed to Pantnagar University of Uttarakhand,

'Sowing of mustard starts in September and continues till end December ... Mustard is a 120-day crop and its harvesting starts from end of December.

If this is correct, then it seems that the sowing and harvesting seasons of mustard overlap: as one group of farm workers finish planting another group starts harvesting.

And, in this cycle, the needs of both Indian and western cuisine converge giving dark green *sarsoo ka saag* for the north Indian *thali* as well as tangy yellow paste for the mustard pot. Which brings us back to the Christmas party: bright with streamers, radiant with the Crib depicting the birth of Jesus. Mustard is not the only spice that plays a prominent, therapeutic, role in these feasts and festivities. So do cloves studding the ham.

And then there are those intriguingly aromatic twins, tightly packaged by nature, clinging intimately, protectively, to each other.

Mustard plant ready for harvest

It's a gem of the Spice Wars.

Children sing it, mumble it, and dance to it without knowing its secret meaning. It goes like this, artfully concealing its historic message behind seemingly innocuous prattle:

> I had a little nut tree,
> Nothing would it bear
> But a silver nutmeg
> And a golden pear.
>
> The King of Spain's daughter
> Came to visit me.
> And all for the sake
> Of my little nut tree.

This apparent bit of doggerel, created in 1797, hides the tale of the spice wars of the 17th century and beyond.

We believe that The Little Nut Tree refers to Arthur, the son of the English king Henry VII. Back in the 15th century, the royal families of England and Spain had got tired of squabbling for spices in the far corners of Asia. There were enough spices in the world to keep both nations happy provided that they could ease out the troublesome Portuguese and Dutch. A suitable marriage could do the trick. If the sixteen-year-old Prince Arthur, heir-apparent to the English throne, could marry the fifteen-year-old Catherine of Aragon, a Spanish princess, it would build a bridge between the two nations. The combined might of England and Spain could then oust the arrogant Iberians and the meddlesome Netherlanders from the spice-rich lands of Asia, and monopolise

Fruit hang on a
Nutmeg tree

Facing page:
Canterbury Cathedral:
West Front, Nave and
Central Tower

NUTMEG AND MACE

the trade. The first part of the plan worked. Arthur and Catherine got married and everyone sat back and expected that, in the fullness of time, Catherine would produce an heir to both thrones. The pact would be sealed in blood.

Sadly, this didn't happen because Arthur died within a year of his marriage.

That was a setback but *realpolitik* never gives in. The two royal families then decided that the young widow, Catherine, should be engaged to her brother-in-law, Henry, who was only eleven years old at the time. Everyone waited patiently. On the death of his father in 1509, Henry was crowned Henry VIII, and, as a dutiful son, married his brother's widow. But though he and Catherine had five children, Henry never seemed to accept the fact that he had been forced to marry Arthur's relict. Besides, the king had a roving eye and he'd spotted a comely lass named Anne Boleyn.

He revolted and demanded that the head of his church, the Pope, permit him to divorce his wife. The Pope refused. Enraged, Henry VIII rejected the Pope's authority and proclaimed the independence of his Church of England.

Many other churches followed and the Reformation was born. Christians were divided between Catholics who still accepted the authority of the Pope, and Protestants who protested their independence.

Instead of closing the gap between England and Spain, the forced marriage, and its vexatious end, widened it. This led to increasingly bitter Protestant-Catholic feuds all over Britain, and the rest of Europe, coming to a head in the late 18th century when the spice wars in Asia had repercussions at home.

The English had ousted the Dutch from Indonesia's Moluccas and Sri Lanka, broken the Netherlanders' ruthlessly enforced monopoly of nutmeg and mace. Among the chattering classes of England, this became the most gleeful topic of the year. It was a welcome change from the gloomy news across the borders. The Irish and the Scots were agitating against English rule. The French revolutionaries, who had guillotined their king and queen, had declared war on England. And the growing middle class, fattening on the trade and plunder of the East India Company, met in Lloyd's Coffee House and said, "*If only the Anglo-Spanish marriage had worked out, things would have been so much better."*

In those days, nursery rhymes served the same purpose that political cartoons do today. They expressed the opinions of civil society in a tongue-in-cheek sort of way. *The Little Nut Tree* was the Prince of Wales, Arthur, who had not fathered a child in spite of the fact that he had a *Silver Nutmeg and a Golden Pear.* We shall not elaborate on that description except to say that *Pear* was probably a pun in the bawdy usage of those times.

Not everyone who uses a nutmeg is aware of the significance of the rhyme. Every Christmas, without thinking about

Various stages of separation of Nutmeg and Mace

history, we grate nutmeg seeds to give a warm, slightly bitter, taste to, our sugar-dusted doughnuts. Sometimes we add a pinch of mace to give the hint of an intriguing flavour to a pudding. We are following a tradition that dates back to the 14th century. Chaucer, in his *Canterbury Tales*, had mentioned nutmeg. It had reached Scandinavia even earlier, as far back as the 12th century, and it is still a popular spice among the people of those cold lands. They brought their tastes to the New World when their families migrated to the USA. So popular did the spice become in North America that unscrupulous Yankee traders, carrying bags of their goods on their backs, had wood carved into little fake nutmegs, soaked them in Nutmeg oil, and peddled them as the real thing. To this day Connecticut is known as *The Nutmeg State* in recognition of its spice scamsters.

By the 19th century, the innovative British had broken Asia's monopoly of nutmeg and mace. They had set up nutmeg plantations in their colonies in the tropics of the Western Hemisphere: in St Vincent, Trinidad and on Grenada. All of them have sheltered valleys not far from the sea, a moist, tropical climate,

NUTMEG AND MACE

and well-drained soil rich in humus. Seeds germinate in about six weeks and the tree does not produce fruit till the seventh year. But it is only a year earlier that the farmer will be able to distinguish between the low-yielding male tree and the highly productive female. One male tree can pollinate ten females, provided he is on the windward side of his harem. But farmers don't have to destroy all male trees. They can graft female scions onto the males. So far no bleeding-heart arborists have protested against these gender-cloning operations on these soaring, shiny-leafed, trees.

We didn't have to go to South-east Asia or the West Indies to see our first nutmeg tree. We had driven out of the warm Arabian Sea beaches of Kochi heading for the forested mountains of Tamil Nadu. Our destination was the blue hills of the Nilgiris where we had a week-long lecture engagement in the Defence Services' Staff College, Wellington. At the little hamlet of Burlier, we had had to give our gasping old car an R&R stop. Burlier is a pretty little wayside station with two temples on the forested slopes, waterfalls, snack stalls, and a long row of open-fronted fruit, vegetable and spice

Facing page: A roadside stall in Burlier, in the Nilgiri Range, displays its freshly harvested offerings including yellow-green Nutmeg fruit

Left: Nutmeg tree laden with fruits

Spices as home decor: A traditional shelf in the dining room of the authors. The cock motif expresses the invigorating power of spices

A bowlful of
nutmeg. Patisseries
use its distinct
flavour to perfection

NUTMEG AND MACE

shops. We were fascinated. Spices hung in shimmering garlands of small plastic packets. There were baskets of fresh green pepper, bottles of cardamom, star anise, cinnamon, clove, ginger, garlic and turmeric. Also shelves stacked with fleshy yellow fruit that looked like apricots but were, clearly, something else. We asked the vendor what they were.

"Nutmeg," he mumbled laconically.

The fruit, he explained, cutting open one of them, splits when it is ripe to reveal a shiny brown shell clasped in a scarlet web of mace much like a tiny octopus embracing a small, un-husked, coconut.

Women removing Mace from Nutmeg

Above left: Within the fruit, a scarlet net of Mace grips the Nutmeg

Above right: Nutmeg peeping out from the fruit and the Mace net

Inside the shell is the glistening brown, egg-shaped, nutmeg.

We learnt, later, that nutmeg farmers have the mace removed from the shell, very carefully and usually by women. It is then dried, gradually, in the sun and slowly, as it turns brittle and yellowish brown, it acquires its distinctive fragrance. The nutmeg seeds are then also dried for about one or two months till the kernel, the real nutmeg, rattles in the shell. The shell is cracked open and, at long last, the nutmeg emerges.

Herbal doctors attribute many medicinal properties to nutmeg including its reputed aphrodisiacal qualities. Chanakya, an ancient Indian master of statecraft, claims that enemies can be killed by giving them an infusion of nutmeg leaves. Modern science says that the essential oils of nutmeg and mace contain about 4 per cent of the very toxic myristicin which, in large amounts, can lead to degeneration of the liver. People who find it difficult to face reality eat two or three tablespoons of powdered nutmeg to get a 'mind-blowing' experience. They wake up to headaches, dizziness and nausea.

We prefer to use it in moderation, dusting it on doughnuts and puddings, on cold winter evenings, agreeing with a friend's

Above left:
Harvesting Nutmeg

Above right: A harvest of Mace

The fruit, the scarlet web of Mace and the Nutmeg inside on a bed of leaves captures the eye and makes one marvel at the beauty and bounty of nature

"

NUTMEG AND MACE

advice. He is addicted to puns and one of his most anguished play on words is: "*Only nuts eat too much of the nut which is why they go nuts.*" If he had lived in the late 18th century, he might even have created a nursery rhyme.

For all his skilled verbal jugglery, however, he could not have got into the world's most widely revered, and very ancient book, **The Holy Bible**.

The seed we now turn to has made it to that powerful bestseller, over and over again.

Dried Nutmeg

Above: Spices proudly displayed in a wayside shop in Kerala

From the Gardens
of Babylon

CUMIN

The world's most revered book is a historic guide to spices.

It is also the bedrock of three Semitic religions and is referred to as *the book*: The Bible. The influence of the Bible comes out clearly in *John W. Parry's* classic *The Story of Spices*. His opening paragraph says:

> *In the beginning, untouched and undisturbed save by the hand of God, the cumin and the anise of Egypt gave up their scent to the gentle Mediterranean breezes which cooled that arid land.*

Written in the style of the first book of the Bible, *Genesis*, Parry gives the impression that the use of spices is at least as old as civilisation. He's right. Cumin was, probably, one of the medicinal spices used by the Babylonians, in southern Mesopotamia, from the early 2nd millennium BC. At that time, aromatic spices were employed largely to perfume and fumigate places where 'noxious and evil vapours' were likely to arise. Before the 18th century scientist, *Louis Pasteur*, discovered that microorganisms breed in unhygienic places and cause disease, mankind rightly associated foul smells with sickness. They tried to counteract these foetid odours by fumigating the area with the fragrant smoke of incense.

The *Incense Route*, linking India and West Asia, dated back to the 3rd century BC and was the world's first international trade route. Using dhows and camels, it reached across the Arabian Sea and the Arabian desert, trading gold, frankincense, myrrh and cumin between the nations of the

A close-up of Cumin clusters

Facing page:
Cumin field promising a lush crop

Dried Cumin is an essential
ingredient of Indian cooking and
seasoning. It is renowned for its
digestive and curative properties. It is
used as a whole spice, as a powder
and also in the spice drop form

C U M I N

then civilised world. India has always been, as it still is, a great consumer of incense. It is more than likely that cumin was brought into India as incense but, thanks to the innovative compulsions of our royal chefs, we seem to have been the first country in the world to have used cumin as a spice, to enhance the flavour of our cuisine. It is mentioned in one of the foremost books on statecraft. The *Arthashastra* was written by Chanakya, wily adviser to the Emperor Chandragupta Maurya who ruled between 321 and 297 BC. In it Chanakya directs the Superintendent of Spices to collect taxes on condiments such as pepper, ginger and cumin.

It was only in the 1st century AD, however, that we find a reference to cumin being eaten in the west. The Roman scholar

Pliny says that, of all the condiments, cumin is the best. But as he recommends it as an appetiser it was still commended for its therapeutic qualities, not for its flavour. It was not until the Middle Ages in Europe that we find cumin being appreciated for its warm flavour, though it was still wreathed in a little magic. There was a curious belief that it kept lovers from straying and poultry from wandering away. Cumin probably refreshed the breath of lovers in an age when halitosis must have been the rule rather than the exception. And since the sweet fragrance of cumin kept lovers together then, by sympathetic magic, cocks and hens would also stay at home!

This could also have been a blurred perception of Ayurvedic lore trickling

Dried Cumin with stalks ready for cleaning

in from India. It was, reputedly, one of the many ingredients in an aphrodisiacal confection called *Kameshwara Modaka*, prescribed for newlyweds. Sadly its recipe has been lost, or perhaps it still lies at the bottom of some ancestral chest waiting to release its potency on eager mankind!

It is more than likely, however, that cumin was still being imported into both India and Europe from the dry lands of West Asia. Then, the wise Mughal Emperor Akbar must have realised that India has all the climates, terrains and soil conditions found across the world. During the fifty years of his reign from the mid-16th to the early-17th centuries, he encouraged the cultivation of temperate spices in his Punjab domains. This is borne out by the detailed records in the famed *Ain-i-Akbari*

compiled by his loyal Prime Minister, Abul Fazal. After describing the banquets that the Emperor's chefs produced every day from a menu spanning the cuisines of many countries, he specifies the spices used in some of the dishes. Cumin seed was used in the vegetarian *Pahit,* the 'mixed' *Qabuli, Bughra, Qima Shurba* and *Kushk,* and the non-vegetarian *Biryani, Kabab, Do Piyaza* and *Mutanjana.* Like all Mughlai dishes, they all sound very delectable but as our culinary skills rise only to *Biryani, Kabab* and *Do Piyaza* we can't comment on the others.

Those interested in finding out more about these dishes should remember that, in India, we call cumin *jeera* or *zeera.* For some strange reason, when the Swedes say *kummin* they're not referring to *cumin*

but to its relative, *caraway*. Their term for *cumin* is *spiskummin*. When the Germans, too, say '*Kummel*' they really mean *caraway*. Now that we have tried to clear the fog from varied names of these two spices, we shall talk about one of the world's most ancient spiced liqueurs. No one knows where, exactly, it originated in Europe but the favourite is Holland. According to one of our encyclopaedias of alcoholic drinks:

> 'Certainly it was being made in Holland in the 1500s and it very much fits the image of such drinks of the time, in that it would have been an unrefined grain spirit masked by an aromatic ingredient.'

The Dutch word for *cumin* is *komijn* which sounds very much like *cuminm*. So, logically, the 'aromatic ingredient' in the great liqueur called *kummel* should be *cumin*. Sadly it's not. The ingredient is *caraway seeds*. So what's the Dutch word for *caraway*? It is *karwij*. Confused? That makes three of us!

We'll move on to something simpler.

Cumin needs a mild, fairly even, climate and has a growing season of about three or four months. Experts tell us that it prefers a rich soil of sandy loam because it does not like being water-logged. Moreover, it does not appreciate shade because it is a native of Upper Egypt and the eastern Mediterranean. Remember, Akbar realised that it would do well in his Punjab region and he was right. It is likely

Facing page: A farmer harvesting Cumin

Right: After threshing, Cumin seeds are dried

Flowering Cumin

CUMIN

to grow to a height of about fifty cms, or perhaps a little taller. Its stem will give out a number of slim branches with long, divided, green leaves and will then produce tiny white or rosy flowers. From these, fruit will form, slightly smaller than an adult's little finger nail. These should then be dried and threshed.

Or, as The Bible puts it:

> For the fitches are not threshed with a threshing instrument, neither is a cart wheel turned upon the cumin; but the fitches are beaten out with a staff, and the cumin with a rod.

Fitches are pulses or dals and the great book recommends that they should be threshed by being beaten, presumably to prevent the seeds from being crushed.

The botanical name of the cumin is *Cuminum cyminum* and it belongs to the *Umbelliferae* family along with *celery* and *carrots*. That vegetative clan does not include a spice which the Iranians call Black Cumin. Its seeds are smaller and have a sweeter fragrance than that of the *cumin* we know. Spice guru Frederic Rosengarten Jr says that Black Cumin grows wild in West Asia especially in the

mountains of south-eastern Iran. But, according to him, it 'is not important as an export crop.' Possibly. One of our staff, who is from the mountains of Garhwal, has just given us two dishes flavoured with tiny black seeds that are smaller and have a sweeter fragrance than cumin. We feel it might be a Himalayan relative of the Iranian *Black Cumin*.

For the present, however, we must move on to another certified spicy member of the *Umbelliferae clan*.

The attendant in this spice shop in Dubai told us that Cumin is used as a condiment, a perfume and an incense

The Greeks Had a Bad Word for it

CORIANDER

It bugged the Greeks.

More specifically, it annoyed one ancient Greek. The scholar Pliny seems to have endorsed his countrymen's view that this spice had the odour of bedbugs: *koris*. We completely disagree with him and his fellow citizens. They might have brought civilisation to the inhabitants of the western world but their sense of smell must have been askew. Coriander does not have a foetid odour. In fact, its fragrance is pleasant and appetizing. Sometimes we eat its fresh, green, leaves between slices of bread and butter like water-cress. In fact even our budgerigars, those perky little Australian parakeets who have been in our family for more than seven decades, enjoy it and come screeching and flying down from their perches when they see us bringing it to their aviary . They pass the succulent stems through their beaks, happily crushing the green sap out of the *Coriandrum*

Budgerigars love coriander, especially the juicy stalk

sataivum, delighting in the *Linalool* which is the active principle of coriander and, presumably, gives it its distinctive taste.

Since our budgies are not insect eaters, clearly they don't find any bedbug taste in the herb.

Or perhaps, the coriander with the distinctive bed bug taste is Greek coriander. We know that tea grown in the same estate but on different locations, and also different seasons, varies in flavour. Pliny really should have tried Indian Coriander before approving of its obnoxious name.

Finally, both Rosengarten and Pliny speak of coriander seed, not of its fresh, green, leaves. In India we use both the seeds and the leaves, each for its own distinctive purpose.

Not all Greeks, however, were averse to coriander. Hippocrates, the wise doctor who lived 400 years before Christ, and

"Pontikonisi", a small island located opposite to "Kanoni". The location is about 5 kms from the centre of Corfu city, Corfu Island, Greece

Green Coriander
leaf, popularly used in
Indian cuisine

CORIANDER

after whom the famed *Hippocratic Oath* has been named, acknowledged that coriander had medicinal value. A century later the Romans who, like the British aped Greek culture, valued Coriander as a seasoning.

There are very strong grounds to believe that much of the scientific knowledge attributed to Greek science had been purloined by them from Indian savants. Centuries before Pliny turned up his nose at Coriander, the great Indian grammarian Panini mentions coriander. It could have been used in spiced wines in an age less hypocritical than ours when the enjoyment of alcohol was a social grace. In fact coriander has, traditionally been associated with the good life. In Pompeii, where rich Romans indulged themselves in long sessions of Rest and Recreation, coriander seeds survived a devastating volcanic eruption. Pompeii was the pleasure dome of Rome and, as its surviving mosaics and frescoes prove, was full of seductive women from all over the Roman Empire. There is reason to believe that they, occasionally, followed an old Indian custom of perfuming their bodies, after bathing, by standing straddle-legged over a pot of embers onto which they threw coriander seeds.

The Romans, who like good food, brought it to England when they invaded those misty isles. For a while the English were delighted but with the departure of the

In a roadside market in the heart of India spices, including Coriander, are offered for sale

cohorts, the English reverted to their stodgy boiled meat and cabbage. This insipid cuisine sustained them till the Empire Struck Back and Indian spices reasserted themselves.

Just about the time this happened, we were entertaining a soft-spoken English writer who had specialised in writing about India. So, we were surprised when she asked, over lunch in Kochi, "What is this interesting herb?" We had used green coriander to garnish both the chicken curry and the dal. It was then that we first realised that though the west is familiar with coriander seed, only people of Indian origin use the fresh, green leaves of coriander as a garnish and, sometimes, as a salad. That got us thinking and we dusted out the many old recipe books we had, most of them written in the clear, almost calligraphic, writing of four grandmothers and a few great-grandmothers. These heritage books often made references to the huge staff of servants employed in the old kitchens: the '*baborchis*' from the Urdu *bawarchi* cook, their *masalchi* helpers, the khansamas who shopped for fresh provisions every day, and the *khidmatgars* who waited at table and always had the last say in what the *sahib-memsahib-baba-*

logs wanted. We discovered, then, that the majority of the servants involved in the selection and preparation of the family's meals, were Muslim. This was, possibly, because the Anglo-Indian kitchen was a non-vegetarian one.

So what has all this got to do with coriander? We'll come to that.

The impact of this spice on the Indian market is an example of the many, often subtle, factors that influence the acceptance of particular spices by consumers. Why, for instance, is mustard so popular with Bengalis? Why is pepper not an important ingredient in traditional Malayali cuisine in spite of the fact that Kerala is the greatest pepper-growing area in the country? Such ethnic biases towards specific spices would be a useful subject of research and form a scientific basis for the marketing of such spices to other people who fit similar sociological templates. For instance, if the Bengalis' preference for mustard is based on their fish-rich diet, would other communities with such diets also take to mustard? We have, to a certain extent, been able to trace the factors that led to our Anglo-Indian leaning towards Coriander.

Dried coriander seeds are a 'must-have masala' for authentic Indian cuisine. The inset clusters of green, yet to dry, seeds look like tiny pomegranates

CORIANDER

Coriander was an imported spice before Akbar the Great decided to grow the West Asian herbs in Punjab and break our dependence on imports. The sudden availability of fresh coriander had an immediate impact on Muslim cuisine in India. Since most of our kitchen staff were Muslims, Anglo-Indian cuisine took on a distinctly Mughlai bias with a generous use of both the leaves and seeds of coriander. We liked the flavour of coriander so much that we incorporated it in our much copied Breast Pepper Water or Mulligatawny. We also use coriander seeds in our European-based dishes like Masala Mince. Of late, we have begun to add coriander herbs in our Cutlets and Masala Scrambled Eggs.

Interestingly, the most popular Anglo-Indian snack, flavoured with coriander leaves, is known by three different names. In the east coast it's called *philaurees*, in the north it's referred to as *pakoras*, and in the west it is *bhajiyas* which foreigners sometimes misnamed *bujeas*. This is the term that David Burton uses in his *The Raj at Table*. He describes them as

'small fritters' and starts his recipe with the words '*Grind a bunch of green kotemer.*' This identifies the provenance of his recipe. *Kotemer* or as Anglo-Indians on the west coast prefer to pronounce it '*kotmir,*' refers specifically to the fresh leaves of coriander. It is treated as a spice in its own right as distinct from *dhania,* the name given to the dried seeds of coriander.

We don't know if it is the seeds or the leaves of coriander used to add flavours to European liqueurs. In Greece we drank their famed Ouzo and liked its spicy tang which went well with fish. Coriander was one of its ingredients, according to our host. The practice of adding herbs to wine was started by the Greeks and then spread across the Mediterranean. The dry Noilly Prat is a French wine fortified with herbs including coriander seeds. Sadly, we mislaid the recipe of a French Great-grand Aunt. Her *eau de Carnes* was a multipurpose concoction of spirits and spices. Those who have tasted it said it had a strong coriander flavour and aroma. It was also, reputedly, a very effective liniment for sprains, aches and pains!

That formulation may have required West Asian coriander but one of the great virtues

A field of Coriander with the flowers in full bloom

Nature's artistry
at work. A bee
pollinating a
coriander flower.
The inset bunch of
flowers is a picture
in contrast

"

CORIANDER

of this spice is that it is very adaptable. It likes the sun and the sandy-loamy soil that its relatives, carrots, prefer and needs fairly good drainage but it also demands evenly-spaced moisture. At one time it thrived only in the dry conditions of Punjab, but, happily for us, it has adapted wonderfully.

According to spice authority, Rosengarten, coriander seeds should be planted in rows in early spring and will mature in about four months. It should be harvested in July or August. The plants should be cut either early in the morning, or late in the evening, when there is dew so that the seeds don't shatter. It is only after the seeds have been thoroughly dried that they should be threshed. Having read that, we were very surprised when one of the couples on our staff asked if they could clean and

Dried Coriander seeds

till a little patch of land behind the staff quarters. It is covered with brambles, nettles and stones and is bordered by a dry ravine. It seemed to be a most unlikely place for cultivation of any sort. We asked them what they wanted to plant.

"*Dhania*."

"But isn't this the wrong time?"

"Not if we want green *dhania*." They called it *hara dhania*, and then emphasised "We don't want *dhania* seeds."

Just then a group of rhesus monkeys leapt through our oak forest. "How will you protect your *dhania* from monkeys?" we asked. Tribes of those marauding simians devastate our flower garden and little orchard, descending like a plague of vicious, brown, imps.

Fresh green Coriander seeds hanging down in clusters, ready to be harvested and dried

CORIANDER

Our prospective coriander farmers smiled. "The *bunder log* don't like the taste and smell of *dhania*," they said. We wondered if the monkeys, like that ancient Greek with his very sensitive palate, were bugged with coriander!

Then we moved on to the third in the carrot-celery family with a reversal of the seed-leaf role. Its seeds are favoured in India for many aromatic and flavoursome reasons, its feathery green leaves are preferred in the west.

Coriander clusters laid out for drying and threshing

*The Wreath
of Gladiators*

FENNEL

Once upon a time, it was a *videshi* spice.

Today, however, it's as Indian as curry. We recall the TV ad that brought this out very clearly. There's this rather starchy young man: tie, ramrod-straight back, dark suit, stern expression. He orders a pizza and proceeds to eat it with a knife and fork. Then his expression changes. He rubs his hands together, puts aside the cutlery, and eats the rest of the pizza with his fingers. Later, obviously contented, he pushes back his chair, summons the waiter, and asks for that traditional gourmet flourish to a good Indian meal: *saunf.*

No other culinary system that we know of has quite the same spicy finale. The customary digestive biscuits of Britain are stodgy by comparison. Liqueurs are a sophisticated substitute but not served

as a matter of course. Jet Air, in its heyday, was the first to offer its passengers what they called, with oh-so-precious affectation, *After Mints.* It was, really, a sweetened *saunf* and foreigners liked it, after they had got over their initial apprehensions.

In fact, foreigners had given it its other name: *Fennel.* That's the short form of *Foeniculum:* 'fragrant hay'. According to a legend, when the powerful Roman cavalry found that their horses did not want to eat hay which had been stored for too long, and had gone sour, they added fragrant fennel hay to the fodder and their valuable steeds ate it with relish. But if this story gives the impression that fennel was discovered by hungry horses, it would be wrong. Long before the martial

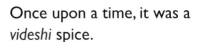

Fennel, the after-meals mouth-freshner

Facing page: A tray of saunf

FENNEL

Romans set about conquering the known world with their legions, fennel had been accepted by a far more ancient, and very much more sophisticated, people: the Chaldeans of Babylon. During the reign of the great ruler, Nebuchadnezzar, from 630 to 562 BC, the towering Hanging Gardens of Babylon had been created. This stupendous structure of terraces, rising on successive arches, was a man-made forested mountain. On it the Chaldeans had nurtured flowering plants and trees from all over the known world. They had also grown about two hundred varieties of spices and herbs because they were skilled herbal-doctors. Among these herbs was fennel.

Sadly, this great treasure trove of ancient lore was destroyed by the savage hordes that invaded and destroyed Babylon when, as all empires do, it became weak and aged. Great knowledge has, however, a dogged way of surviving though it might get a bit distorted in its passage down the centuries. Blurred beliefs of the curative powers of fennel had trickled down to the Greeks. It became their symbol of success. In 490 BC, after they had scored a decisive victory over the Persians in Marathon, they called fennel *marathon*. It was, however, left to

> Fennel plants thriving in a lush field. A close-up of the clusters proclaims it to be a relation of cumin

FENNEL

their cultural successors, the Romans, to rediscover the many qualities of this herbal spice. These sybaritic people, revelling in the wealth of their empire, gave the world the term *la dolce vita,* 'the good life'. They used fennel to spice their wines and to add piquancy to their sauces. The fact that it also helped them to digest their gourmand meals was an added advantage. Though hedonism seemed to be the major concern of the rich citizens of Rome, in those heady days of the Empire, there was a significant sprinkling of scholars who, like true scientists and philosophers, observed the world around them and drew conclusions about why things happened the way they did.

Among these thinkers was a man named Pliny. When he saw snakes sloughing off their old skin, after their winter hibernation, he also noted that they nibbled on the juicy stems of spring-green fennel. Snakes are normally thirsty after their long winter sleep and fennel would be a good source of moisture. Though his observation was correct, his conclusion was wrong. He said that snakes use fennel to improve their eyesight when they emerge into the sun from the dark of their burrows.

Though medicine has always had an element of faith and magic in it, now referred to as the placebo effect, folk beliefs often precede scientific discovery. The beneficial effects of fennel on the eyesight is a belief that has persisted through the ages and we shall come back to it as we pick up the flavours of fennel wafting down the centuries.

The intermingling of scholarship and faith was focused in the great monasteries of the Middle Ages. The monks, alone, had the time and the facilities to study, research and compare notes with each other. Often, they were the only literate people in the region. Their herbal gardens catered to the people of the towns and villages around them, as well as to travellers. They provided lodgings for the tired and sick. From these hospices evolved the word hospital. Very often, the fame of the herbal gardens encouraged their rulers to start spice plantations of their own. The powerful Emperor Charlemagne encouraged the cultivation of spices, between AD 742 and 814 and had fennel grow in his royal gardens.

Over the centuries, as more and still more spices flowed into Europe along the *Incense Route,* these aromatic substances

Facing page:
A field of feathery Fennel

spread out beyond the royal gardens and monasteries. Guilds of spice merchants established themselves and, as all traders do, encouraged beliefs in the efficacy of their exotic products. They recommended, and concocted, the spice-fortified *Wine of Tyre* or *Tiberias* which included fennel. It was a specific for ailments of the chest. Then there was that other all-purpose powder of fennel and thirteen other spices which will:

Cleanse the brain, do away with headaches, clarify the sight, aid the digestion and destroy wind.

Though this sounds very much like some of the claims made by *jari-booti* peddlers in village *haats,* we're wary about dismissing their claims. Every spice has some medicinal virtues and when you mix them all together they might have a panacea effect. After all, we take multi-vitamin capsules, don't we?

In the 14th century another interesting trend emerges. Fennel seeds begin to be sugared and eaten as a confection. Had our custom of eating a mixture of sugar-candy and *saunf* as a digestive come to us from Europe, or was it the other way around? Then from the herbal book of the

Rural housewives
threshing Fennel

Above: A woman
harvesting Fennel

A jungle like growth of Fennel plants

English doctor, John Gerard, we learn that the powdered seed of fennel preserves the eyesight. The fine, green, thread of fennel lore, first spun by Pliny's opinion that snakes improve their hibernation-weakened eyesight by eating fennel, has stretched down the centuries and emerged as a fortifier of human vision too.

The association of fennel with light and vision occurs so often in folklore that there should be more than a grain of truth in it. The Greeks claimed that when the Olympian god Zeus deprived mankind of fire, because he was furious with them, his cousin Prometheus stole sparks from the wheel of the sun, hid them in the stalks of giant fennel, and restored fire to the world. The pithy stalks of fennel were often used as tinder to start fires from sparks produced by striking stones together. Then there was John Milton's praise of fennel. This 17th century English writer authored the epic *Paradise Lost* in 1667, sixteen years after he became blind. Relying on his other senses he wrote of the *smell of sweetest fennel*. He must have been familiar with the fragrance because

FENNEL

his fellow Puritans were fond of chewing it in church and called it 'the meetin' seed.' Two centuries later, American Poet Henry Wadsworth Longfellow spoke of its rejuvenating power, 'Lost vision to restore,' and claimed that:

"gladiators, fierce and rude,
Mingled it with their daily food;
And he who battled and subdued,
A wreath of fennel wore."

Clearly, fennel was far more popular in the west than in the east. Indian poets, perhaps, can't wax eloquent about digestives! And though we, in our family, also cook its leaves as we would any other green, leafy, vegetable and relish its slightly bitter, aromatic, taste, we are not poets. Besides, we have not, as yet, tried growing it in our garden even though we have its preferred, limy, well-drained loamy soil and a generally mild climate. We might have a shot at it next spring, but that's in the future. Now, having paid our respects to the three cousins of the carrot-celery family we have to move further afield.

The formal name of our next spice translates as 'Greek-hay'. But that's deceptive. These tiny seeds conceal, within themselves, a multitude of exciting possibilities.

Fennel clusters with fruits peeping out of the flower heads

Gourmet Hay

FENUGREEK

Both the ancient Greeks and the Romans liked eating; but there was a difference.

The Greeks were gourmets: they had a delicacy of taste. The Romans, on the other hand, indulged in gorging: the orgies of ancient Rome were legendary. Happily, it is Greek tastes rather than Roman ones that have left a lasting impact on our cuisine. And also on some of our traditional medical systems. *Unani*, the term for the Islamic medical system, is literally *Greek*. The Greeks, in turn, probably learnt about the virtues of subtle tastes from an even earlier civilisation: the Egyptians. Those Pharaonic people knew a great deal about herbs and spices, as an Egyptologist discovered in 1878. In that year, a German named George Ebers unearthed an extraordinary, 20-metre long, papyrus document, now named after him. From the *Ebers Papyrus*, probably written in 1550 BC, we learn that fenugreek was one of the ingredients used by the Egyptians in their cosmetics, ointments, food and incense. Their 'Holy Smoke' was called *kuphi*. It contained a fair amount of fenugreek. It not only helped preserve their embalmed mummies but it also disinfected their houses. Incense smoke produces phenol or carbolic acid, a famed antiseptic. This could account for its use in temples, churches and mosques. The warm, moist, breath of people crowded into confined spaces, provides ideal conditions for the growth of harmful micro-organisms. Carbolic acid, wafted around in incense, helps check the spread of such harmful disease-causing bacteria.

A dragon-theme incense burner from Myanmar. The potter showed us Fenugreek seeds and said that this spice was one of the aromatic ingredients used in the censer

Facing page: A field of Fenugreek with the pods standing out like unsheathed swords

FENUGREEK

Incenses were the original perfumes: the word perfume was derived from the words *per fumare* or 'by smoke'. Fenugreek could soon become the source of an expensive perfume, if this hasn't happened already. Years ago when a Frenchman from the famed perfume industry of Grasse tasted one of our *methi parathas,* he wrinkled his nose like a sensitive rabbit and said "It has possibilities, distinct possibilities, in masculine toiletries. Yes …" another wrinkle of his nose, "and why not? … why not? … for women too?" So the next time you attend a Page 3 party, and smell the fragrance of *methi,* it might not be the hors-d'oeuvre. It could be that slinky model poured into a shimmering designer gown and drenched in *Eau de Fenugrec.*

We are not perfumers, pharmacists or dieticians but for years we have greeted every morning, in our Victorian cottage in the oak woods of the Himalayas, with a gulp of fenugreek. We do this because of the advice given by an old Anglo-Indian friend. Her husband had been an Army doctor who had served in Alexandria.

Fenugreek seeds, soaked overnight, are a traditional breakfast tonic which, reputedly, controls arthritis, high blood pressure and cholesterol

There he had enquired into, and compiled, a list of traditional Egyptian herbal cures. His widow had asked us, "In your job can you afford to get arthritis, diabetes, unruly digestions, headaches and a blurring of the vision?" We admitted that we couldn't. "Then you better start on the *methi preventive*. My hubby swore by it and recommended it to all his friends" Ever since then, we take two half-teaspoons of fenugreek seeds, soak them in a little water overnight and, the next morning, we eat the water-softened seeds and drink the water in which they have been soaked. That was many years ago and we're still travelling, still taking photographs, still writing.

Fenugreek, however, is not only a herbal medicine, it is also a flavouring agent. Its bitter-sweet, slightly smoky taste is used to make artificial maple sugar helping to save those stately trees from having their sap tapped. Closer to home, *Methi-*

aloo, fenugreek greens and potatoes, is a popular northern Indian dish. We've also eaten it in the *Hulba* bread in Egypt and as *Abish* in the Ethiopian hill-station of Asmara when one of us was a Naval officer. The imaginative use of fenugreek in these lands is natural because it is a native of the temperate regions of southern Europe and the Mediterranean. In the Med we have been offered it as an appetite stimulant. Some years ago, we travelled out of Athens on a day-long cruise on the Saronic Gulf. Along with us was a Greek family showing their American friends the sights associated with Homer's sailing epic, the *Odyssey*. Just before lunch they passed around little bowls of what they described as "*an effective restorative*". We were included in their largesse because, as a tanned elder of the family explained, "When I was a young man I was a sailor on an oil tanker which frequently touched Bombay. I developed a taste for *bel puri* eaten at the Parsi Well. This is our *bel puri!*" Their non-alcoholic *aperitif* had a hauntingly familiar taste: it was boiled fenugreek seeds soaked in honey. Our American fellow-travellers were inquisitive.

"What does it do?" asked one of them who looked like a crew-cut football jock.

A tray of Fenugreek seeds

A Fenugreek plant with flowers on the wither and pods ready to be harvested. A close-up shows the sword like pods ripping the flower petals to register their presence

"

FENUGREEK

"Well," rumbled his suave Greek host smoothly, "it keeps up the enthusiasm but keeps down the population."

The jock smiled vaguely, not understanding at all.

The Greek's cryptic remarks gave us a lead. When we returned to India we did a little more research into the properties of this versatile spice. We learnt that a greatly valued, natural chemical, called *diosgenin* is extracted from a slow-growing, wild yam. Pharmaceutical companies use *diosgenin* to manufacture both sex hormones and oral contraceptives. Now, they may no longer have to cultivate the reluctant yam because Fenugreek seeds have been shown to contain the versatile steroid. The Greek elder had described Fenugreek's varied powers in a very Homeric way.

This could also be one reason, or rather two reasons, why West Asian and European women, at one time, consumed fenugreek seeds, encouraged by their husbands. This had an interesting side effect that was reflected in classic art. The voluptuousness of the, so-called, Reuben's figure could have been inspired by the bounteous curves of harem odalisques. Both were, probably, beneficiaries of the

effects of *methi* seeds. In fact some of our own, Indian, communities believe that lactating mothers should include fenugreek in their diet to build bonny babies. This tradition, in all likelihood, originated from the experience of farmers. They found that if the hay that they had set aside for their animal's winter feed went 'sour', the addition of a little straw made from dried *methi* plants sweetened the fodder again. This was a technique that the ancient Greeks used, which is why *methi* came to be called Fenugreek: 'Greek Hay.' This hay, however, gave another unexpected bonus. The milk yield of the fenugreek-eating cattle improved. If hay could work such wonders for cattle surely seeds could benefit humans. Farm-wives had also noticed that when their horses ate *methi* hay their coats became thicker and glossier. Consequently, when they found their husbands '*getting a little thin on top*' they encouraged them to add more *methi* to their diet. To this day many folk believe that *methi* produces a fuzz on even the baldest pate!

Are all these Old Wives' Tales or psycho-somatic placebo effects? They could be either, or both. But when a belief persists from generation to generation then there is likely to be a great deal of truth in it.

Dried Fenugreek seeds. Apart from their use as spices, their medicinal value is also much acclaimed

FENUGREEK

Strangely, however, we have not been able to find any reference to fenugreek in Indian literature before the arrival of the Mughals. It seems that it was only after Akbar the Great decided to grow temperate herbs in his gardens in Lahore that *methi* was introduced to the Indian kitchen.

Fenugreek needs a temperate, Mediterranean-type climate with a low annual rainfall. It also wants loamy soil which is fairly well-drained. Since we, living in the Garhwal Himalayas, can get fresh, green, *methi* in our local markets, it is obviously a commercial crop of this region. In fact one of our staff, who is from the hills, grows *methi* at the base of our lemon trees. She claimed that it provided *khad*, that is, manure or fertiliser, to the trees by its mere presence. "No, it does not have to be ploughed in as green manure," she insisted. "Its living roots give food to the lemon trees." We didn't see how this was possible but since the *methi* couldn't possibly harm the trees because it is a shallow-rooted herb, not more than 50 cm tall, we didn't say anything. The lemon trees did thrive, but that could have been a coincidence. Much later we learnt that fenugreek is a leguminous crop and its roots have little nodules which host nitrogen-fixing bacteria. They *do* enrich the

soil. Out with superstitions and Old Wives Tales, in with botanical wisdom.

The next spice is as multi-talented *as methi*. In addition, *Papaver somniferum* is also very controversial and, in one case, has been banned on religious grounds.

In India, especially in the north, the Fenugreek leaves are welcomed in the winters to be combined with other vegetables and transformed into delightful vegetarian dishes like aloo methi, methi paratha, gajar methi, etc

Beyond Illusions

POPPY SEEDS A.K.A.
KHUS KHUS

This little spice has become famous for all the wrong reasons.

We learnt this many years ago in a rather tangential way. A leading tourism magazine had asked us to write an article on spices. Most of our editors are very kind to us: they don't edit our work, and if they feel that it needs tweaking then they send it back to us, asking us to do it our way. So we were very surprised to see that our article contained something we had neither written nor could vouch for. It said that if a passenger takes poppy seeds, into Saudi Arabia, he'll be prosecuted for carrying narcotics!

We don't say that they won't do it: we also have some rather bizarre laws in our country. But if the Saudis believe that poppy seeds contain any opium, we have news for them. Nature has so structured the poppy flower that no opium can reach the seeds. This is how the *Encyclopaedia Britannica* puts it:

> 'Poppy seeds have no narcotic properties because the fluid contained in the bud that becomes opium is present only before the seeds form.'

Clearly, not all poppy seed consumers know this even though it has been used for many centuries. Poppy seeds have been found in the mud below ancient Swiss Villages. At that time, the ever-cautious Swiss lived in settlements built on stilts rising out of their lakes: secure from wild beasts and often wilder invaders. Even so, they grew poppies and harvested their seeds. In fact, to this day

Poppy pods containing the seeds

the very delectable Swiss pastries are often sprinkled with poppy seeds to add to their flavour.

Even earlier than the Swiss, the Egyptians cultivated poppy. It is one of the medicinal plants listed in the famous *Ebers Papyrus* though then it was not used as a spice but as a sedative. Presumably, therefore, the Egyptians tapped the flower to extract its gum, opium. Since the Greco-Egyptian Ptolemies ruled Egypt from 323 to 30 BC, they could have been the bridge through which the use of poppy seeds crossed into Greece. From then on the Greeks had the most lasting etymological impact on the poppy's sleep-inducing gum. The short form of their word for juice is *opion* which gave us the word opium and the word *morphine,* which is a product of opium, comes from Morpheus, the Greek god of dreams. The juice's narcotic effects are also enshrined in the language of the European culture that succeeded the Grecian: that of the Latin speaking Romans. Poppy's Latin title is *somniferum*, 'the vehicle of sleep', clearly a reference to its narcotic gum. Perhaps this is also why the poppy flower became an emblem of those warriors who had given up their lives for their country and now rest in revered peace in the military graveyards of the world.

We could go on in this vein, writing about the viciously exploitive Opium Wars inflicted by the colonial powers on China, or the Opium Dens that once stupefied sailors in Victorian London, or the fact that opium, in controlled doses, brought relief from the pain of cholera, dysentery and malaria. Physicians, in the 18th and 19th centuries often prescribed the pleasant-tasting codeine, derived from opium, to ease the effects of a *runny tummy.* We are not, however, writing about the narcotic gum of the poppy, but about its seeds used as a condiment and a spice: *Khus Khus.*

Though the Egyptians included the poppy in the *Ebers papyrus* for its medicinal properties, they were also the first people to use *Khus Khus* as a food: they extracted an edible oil from it. We don't know how they used this oil but, today, it is recognised as an excellent salad dressing and it doesn't go rancid as fast as the better-known olive oil. It takes about 9,00,000 seeds to weigh half a kilo which would then yield about 50–60 per cent of oil. Clearly between the commercial value of its oil and the demand for its seeds as a spice, poppy farming is a rewarding activity. There are poppy fields from as far north as Russia to as far south as Argentina. Also in Holland, Poland,

A tray of Indian spices: flavoursome and therapeutic. Inspiring the *Ebers Papyrus*? Poppy seeds were one of the constituents of this tray

"

POPPY SEEDS A.K.A. KHUS KHUS

Iran, Romania, the former Republic of Czechoslovakia now divided into the Czech Republic and Slovakia. There are poppy fields also in our sub-continent where the soil and climatic conditions are favourable.

Poppy plants like a well-manured soil, adequate moisture and plenty of sunshine. Seeds are planted in March so that the flowering plants, growing a metre or more high, stand about 30 cms apart. The flowers, which range from white to mauve, bloom in July and the harvest can begin in September. After the flowers wither the poppy capsule appears. These are harvested when they turn yellow-brown. These are dried and the very tiny *Khus Khus* seeds are then removed. We know that there was a market for them as far back as the 1st century AD, in Rome. Famed scholar Pliny refers to a paste that can be spread on bread. It was made of parched *Khus Khus* and honey and it sounds quite delectable. Another historical use of *Khus Khus* has been recommended by the 2nd century AD Greek physician, Galen. He proposed mixing *Khus Khus* with flour to create a spiced bread. Given the growing global appetite for herbal foods today, these Retro Recipes should have a great future.

From the Greeks and the Romans, the use of *Khus Khus* spread all across Europe in the Middle Ages. At that time, European food was rather tasteless and anything that made meals more flavoursome was welcomed. Later, when the European nations became colonial powers, triggered by their quest for Indian spices, the use of *Khus Khus* declined. Even to this day, however, we have tasted *Khus Khus* in the baked confections of many western nations, especially Switzerland, Italy and France. From there it was carried over the Atlantic to North America. The descendants of those migrant Europeans still use *Khus Khus* to flavour their confections. Interestingly, in Frederic Rosengarten's authoritative *The Book of Spices* we find two recipes for Poppy Seed Filling. Both use *Khus Khus* and Honey, among other ingredients, to create a spread that could well have its origins in Pliny's 1st century recipe.

Curiously, in spite of its popularity in its native lands, from the eastern Mediterranean across into Central Asia, *Khus Khus* seems to have made no impact on early Indian cuisine. The first reference we can find is in the *Ain-i-Akbari* compiled by the Emperor Akbar's Prime Minister Abul Fazl. The Great Mughal had realised

Facing page:
A Swiss bakery in Schaffhausen. We have tasted *Khus-Khus* in the baked confections of many European nations

POPPY SEEDS A.K.A. KHUS KHUS

that his domains in Lahore and Multan were eminently suited for the cultivation of temperate spices which were needed for authentic Mughlai cuisine. *Khus Khus* was one of the spices grown in the royal farms. But was the use of these seeds confined to Islamic kitchens in our land? To answer this question we ploughed through the old Anglo-Indian recipe books in our collection. Our community is a Pan-Indian one: it has never been confined to any one state or region. Because most of our people were in transferable jobs in the

Railways, Posts & Telegraphs, Police and the Defence Services, our cuisine became eclectic, drawing from local sources all across our land. Our housewives adapted dishes produced by cooks drawn from the places where their husbands worked, and adapted these dishes to suit our tastes.

On trolling through our treasured old cook books we found a distinct pattern emerging in the use of *Khus Khus* as a culinary spice. The famed *Mrs. Bartley* included it in her Curry

An Anglo-Indian chicken curry and the many spices that make it so delicious. White Poppy Seeds are in the centre of the tray.

Facing page: Poppy field

POPPY SEEDS A.K.A. KHUS KHUS

Powder. Specifically, however, she used it in her *Moley Curry, Duck Curry and Mussala Fry*. Significantly, she always included either ground coconut or coconut milk in every recipe in which she used *Khus Khus*. This gives us the impression that these recipes also had a coastal bias. In a hand-written exercise book of uncertain vintage, we have our Anglo Indian variations of *Rogan Josh, Shahi Korma and Baghare Baigan*. All three dishes also used *Khus Khus* and are variations of Hyderabadi adaptations of Mughlai cuisine. Interestingly, *Baghare Baigan* is the only vegetarian dish, in our collection, that requires *Khus Khus*. Another famed Anglo Indian chef, *G.L. Routleff*, included *Khus Khus* as an ingredient of her non-vegetarian curries. Her recipe for *Korma*, which is a typical Islamic dish, also has *Khus Khus* as one of its spices. In our generation, with a family tradition of having a rice lunch only on Sundays, the Mughlai *Biryani* in which *Khus Khus* is used, is a favourite. At this stage it seemed to us that *Khus Khus* is a spice that migrated into Indian cuisine from West Asia and, for some obscure reason, was embargoed from the older culinary traditions of our land. Then, as if to underscore the West Asian origin of the use of *Khus Khus* as a culinary spice, we recalled frequent mentions of *Khus*

Khus in our books of Parsi recipes. These very enterprising people fled religious persecution in Iran in the 7th century, and settled on the West Coast. In a covenant that they entered into with a local, Indian, ruler they agreed to adopt certain Indian customs and traditions, their cuisine remained their own, evolving to suit their changing tastes. As might have been expected their iconic dish, the redoubtable *Dhan Sakh* has *Khus Khus* as one of its essential ingredients.

The *bon vivant* Parsis also use another flower-spice in some of their sweets. We get the impression, however, that this expensive spice is included more to colour their confections than to give them a subtle taste. Having said that, we must admit that colour does play a very important role in its allure. Our first sight of a flowering field of this spice, in the soft light of a Himalayan morning, was heart-stopping, clearly the domain of dreamy-eyed poets and lovers.

A Shade Beyond Colour

SAFFRON

SAFFRON

It plays a dual role: as a rare and expensive condiment as well as a distinctive and aspirational colour.

We call the condiment *zafran* from the Arabic word meaning 'yellow'. The colour is known as *kesri* and has acquired a vast range of spiritual and political connotations. Consequently, this delicate flower spice has inspired more myths, legends, customs, traditions and lyrical writing than any other in world history.

In one of mankind's oldest, and most revered love poems, The Bible's *Song of Solomon,* the beloved's body is compared to a fruitful orchard in which many luscious and fragrant plants grow, including saffron. Very evocatively this conjures up both the glow of her body and its delicate but exciting fragrance. The power of the perfume of saffron to invigorate is so much a part of our traditions that many people believe that a pinch of saffron held under the nose, will restore consciousness to a comatose person.

We don't know if this really works but we did have an unforgettable experience of the first sight of this spice.

It happened when we were travelling in Kashmir. Driving out of a valley, we breasted a hump and onto a high plain. There, before us, was an incredible spectacle. The top of the plateau was a flat field stretching all the way to the brown mountains etched by a brilliant morning sun. And between us and the curve of the earth's shoulder was a bluish-purple haze, shot with occasional tinges of orange as the breeze touched it. It looked as if

Red Saffron threads are actually the stamen of the purple Saffron flower. their colour captivates the eye

someone had spread an enormous, fine, watered-silk sheet over the vast hectares of that field; and when a vagrant wind touched it, it fluttered gently, changing colour. From where our car had stopped we had no idea, absolutely no idea, what on earth we were looking at.

In fact, it was distinctly alien, as if a space-warp had conjured up a landscape from another world.

It was only when a shred of cloud drifted over the sun, and the light no longer dazzled us, that we saw that the field was dotted with tiny figures of men and women, bent double, working diligently.

"That's saffron," our guide said. "You're looking at a saffron field." And then he added proudly, "It is one of the most beautiful things you can see in our very beautiful Kashmir. Come, I will show you the saffron flowers."

We picked our way carefully over the rough terrain. The little green daggers of the plants thrust their way out between clods of earth:

Mauve Saffron flowers with their delicate, red stamens

Red threads of Saffron: the world's most expensive spice

Page 212-213: A panoramic view of Srinagar and Dal Lake, Kashmir, India

there seemed to have been no attempt at harrowing this field. The small, sharp, leaves appeared to thrive in the challenge of thrusting their way between the unbroken lumps of earth. Now, on a closer look, little blue blooms struck a distinctly familiar chord. In our cottage in the Himalayas, generally after a thunderstorm at a certain time of the year, bunches of beautiful lily-like flowers start bursting out of our hillsides. Some people call them *Thunder Lilies,* others refer to them as *Wind Flowers* because they nod their delicate heads with every passing breeze. And when they appear, our honey bees get berserk. They buzz out of their hive like attacking squadrons of fighter planes, dive into the flowers, and emerge with their legging-like pollen-sacks yellow and bulging.

Our wild crocuses are pink, the saffron *Crocus sativus* has a blue flower but the pollen-laden stigmas at its heart are an explosive sunset-orange. Blue and orange-red, two colours at the opposite ends of the spectrum, perfectly though extravagantly matched in the world's most flamboyant spice: Saffron.

Naturally, such strikingly beautiful blooms have given rise to a legend of fervid romance and dark tragedy. We had first heard it in our part of the Himalayas.

According to the tale, a Kashmiri ruler was riding through his high domains when, one moonlit night, he heard a woman singing in the saffron fields. Her voice, and the magical setting, so enraptured him that he sent for the woman's husband and ordered him to divorce his wife. The petrified man did as he had been commanded and the besotted king married her. Sadly … or perhaps it was divine retribution … the love-struck ruler was dethroned by an invading Mughal Emperor and spent the rest of his life in exile. The unfortunate woman, deprived of two husbands, lost her mind and, distraught, wandered through the saffron fields singing mournful songs about her cruel fate. No one knows when she died, or where she was buried or if, like a wilted saffron flower, she withered and died and her dust continues to be blown across the saffron fields making the flowers nod their heads in sadness. But there are people who say that, on moonlit nights, when the wind whispers down from the high mountains, the covetous king's horse can still be heard neighing above the keening voice of the star-crossed woman.

The unreal beauty of the saffron fields lend themselves to such other-worldly tales.

Even the planting of the saffron corms was, traditionally, wrapped in mystique. Saffron farmers, we were told, started their agricultural season by making a pilgrimage to Zawan spring near Palampur. There, after the appropriate ceremonies, they poured milk into the waters of the oracular spring. If the milk sank the saffron crop would be good; but if it floated, the *Crocus sativus* would not thrive. It is easy to ridicule such beliefs but we believe that if there was no truth in them, successive generations would have forgotten them. Springs are fed by underground water which, presumably, also irrigates the roots of saffron lilies. If the aquifers are charged with snow-melt, making the water in the spring circulate with currents, the roots of the saffron plants will be well nourished. But if the water in the spring is still, because water is not gushing in, saffron plants will be deprived of moisture. The movement of the milk in the Zawan spring is an augury of the future of the saffron crop.

This dependence on environmental conditions was remarked upon by the Mughal Emperor Jehangir. We have come across an unauthenticated but seemingly accurate quotation from his memoirs which speaks about his experience in the saffron fields of Kashmir. He is reputed to have written:

'This land is not ploughed or irrigated: this plant springs up among the clods.'

SAFFRON

And then he adds a curious aside:

> 'When plucking the flowers, all my attendants got headaches from its sharp scent. Though I drink wine and took a cup, I too got a headache. I asked the Kashmiris, who were employed in picking up flowers, how they felt. I understand that they had never experienced a headache in their lives.'

Perhaps the scent of saffron, wafting up from an entire field, could trigger a migraine when inhaled for the first time. When, however, it is absorbed in small quantities over an entire growing season, the farmers' bodies build up an immunity to the chemicals in the perfume. Curiously, or perhaps not so curiously, the oils of saffron, which give it its distinctive perfume, contain a chemical called *crocin*. That, to us, rings an analgesic bell.

Similar references to saffron dot the pages of history. We know that saffron was grown in Egypt and in the legendary

Saffron fields are characterised by their untilled texture. The flowers in bloom spread a purple carpet and a near-divine fragrance

Hanging Gardens of Babylon. The Romans, wallowing in the wealth of their empire, scattered saffron straw in their festive halls, burnt it to perfume their homes, even bathed in saffron water. The saffron-growing nations of West Asia tried to impose an embargo on the export of saffron corms but, as generally happens, this was broken by an enterprising visitor who smuggled a corm in his hollowed pilgrim staff, into England. That was the beginning of the thriving saffron farms of Essex near a town later named Saffron Walden. We have not, however, been able to find out why saffron farmers were then known as *crokers*. Were sore throats an occupational hazard of these growers because they had to hunch over charcoal fires when drying the precious stigmas of the flowers?

Saffron plants need a temperate climate, well-drained, sandy-loamy soil. When the plants begin to bloom, the flowers may last for only two weeks. During that time the three delicate stigmas in each small flower must be hand-plucked immediately after the flowers open. Seventy thousand flowers should produce about three times that number of tiny stigmas and these lose 80 per cent of their weight when dried. As soon as they have been dried they have

to be stored in containers, protected from light, otherwise they will bleach and lose their value. When ready for the market they are a fragrant, brownish-orange mass of strands about 2.5 cms long. This labour-intensive, light-weight, floral product is, naturally, the world's most expensive spice.

This could account for the fact that, traditionally, saffron is used in pinches rather than in spoonfuls. The flavour of saffron is an essential part of Mughlai dishes. In their *Biryani*, lamb, nuts and spices are cooked along with rice flavoured and coloured with saffron. Derived from Islamic dishes but unsuitable for followers of the Prophet is *Pork Korma* which also calls for saffron. Naturally *Murg Kashmiri* coming from the home of Indian saffron would demand the golden spice. What does come as a surprise to us, however, is the use of this spice in that sinfully delectable yoghurt confection *Shrikhand*. We have always associated this sweet with Maharashtra and saffron is not a popular spice in their cuisine. We now learn that it could have been a favourite of the Nawabs of Gujarat who would have been biased towards Mughlai food. Maharashtra and Gujarat together formed the province of Bombay in the days of the British Empire.

All of which goes to underscore the fact that cuisine is an evolving, eclectic art that bridges social barriers effortlessly leading to a seamless integration of tastes. In fact, in Kashmir we saw a wonderful example of how food is sensitive to those societal boundaries that cannot be breached. In the beautiful valley of Srinagar we were invited to a traditional *Wazwan* banquet. In a tribute to democratic camaraderie, diners sat at tables for four with little dishes of meat and vegetables before them and a huge platter of steaming biryani in the centre of the table. Diners were expected to help themselves to the biryani, digging into the same platter. Islamic tradition decrees that guests should serve themselves from the same platter using their fingers, or cutlery, that their hosts use to feed themselves. There were no separate serving spoons. But Hindu custom considers it anathema to 'pollute' another person's food with your 'soiled' fingers or used cutlery. This conflict of customs was solved admirably. The central platter of biryani was quartered into four by distinctive lines of saffron. Guests delved only into the segments demarcated for them!

Moreover, since saffron has a strong religious significance for many people, the spiritually cauterising effect was further reinforced.

Which brings us to the porous membrane between *zafran* and *kesri*: the condiment and the colour.

The reddish-yellow pigment of the spice is so strong that one part will stain one hundred and fifty thousand parts of water. But *kesri* has gone a shade beyond colour. Because a little bit covered a lot, it was an inexpensive dye and, therefore, suitable for those who had renounced the world. It was adopted by Vedic hermits, anchorites and monks as the colour for their identifying robes. And since this striking colour also evokes the aspirational and purifying glow of sunrise, it has become the colour of spiritual achievement and self sacrifice. Today, it proudly flies on the top one-third of our National Flag: an icon of our determination to secure for our nation its rightful place in the sun.

While we have such elevated thoughts, this is the appropriate time to consider the delicate flavour produced by a really exotic flowering plant. It's an orchid which is so fastidious that, in our land, it needs human help to nurture it, cosset it and even to get it to propagate.

*From the Halls
of Montezuma*

VANILLA

VANILLA

Christmas in our cottage in the woods of the Himalayas, is Vanilla Time.

We, as the youngest of India's mosaic of 4635 communities, have taken the youngest international spice to our hearts, and kitchens. We use vanilla in our Christmas cakes, chocolate cakes, sponge cakes, eggnogs, custards and even in a secret non-alcoholic tipple called OT, the Other Thing. Not all Anglo-Indians use vanilla in their OTs but the virtue of our OT is that one can match *Cheers!* for *Cheers!* with the most dedicated Bacchus in the community … which is saying a lot … without feeling that you've been 'water-boarded' in a secret CIA facility!

This quality of vanilla must have got the Aztec Emperor of Mexico hooked to vanilla before he entertained Hernan Cortes and his Spanish conquistadores

to his fabled Hall of Audience in 1520. There he was all decked out in his quetzal plumes and gold, sitting on his golden throne, gazing in wonder at these pale-faces clamped into their metal helmets and metal cuirasses and metal armour clanking around the place and sweating in the tropical heat of Mexico. '*Surely they are an effete race*' thought the Emperor, '*to feel cold in this heat!*' And so, out of the generosity of his heart, he offered them *chocolatl*. And when one of the other pale faces, a *hidalgo* named Bernal Diaz, asked, "What is it?" the Emperor told his royal barman to reveal his recipe. It was a beverage made of powdered cocoa beans and ground corn flavoured with *tlilxochitl* and honey. Diaz was zapped. Not only could he not

The Vanilla vine

Facing page: The flavour of chocolate, as in this cake, is enhanced by Vanilla: a combination first discovered by Amerindians

pronounce *tlilxochitl*, he still hadn't a clue
what it was. And so the royal barman told
the assistant barman who told the head
waiter who told the scullery boy who
told the sub-assistant-under-gardener's-
daily-wager help to show this questing
paleface a *tlilxochitl*. Which is how the
first European saw the first Vanilla pods.

And that, to cut a long story of invasion,
plunder and exploitation short, is how
vanilla reached Europe. A similar tale was
crafted by the first cousins of the Spanish,
the Iberian Portuguese, with the Zamorin
of Calicut in Kerala. The difference was
that Vasco da Gama's *fidalgos* took back
pepper, not vanilla. The descendants of
those Portuguese pillagers are still using
pepper as the descendants of those
Spanish conquistadores are still using
vanilla to flavour their chocolate.

We had a firsthand experience of this
four centuries after Bernal Diaz learnt
that *tlilxochitl* was ground black vanilla
pods. We were relaxing in a chocolate
bar in Madrid. The shop leading to the bar
offered an unbelievable array of exotically
flavoured chocolates including one that
tasted of fish (intriguing) and another of
'curry' (nostalgic). In the back-room bar
we were offered mugs of sweet, creamy,

thick chocolate with cinnamon quills as stirrers. The richness of the chocolate was brought out by vanilla in the same way as Montezuma's barman had done, many centuries ago, for Bernal Diaz.

The canny Bernal, however, had not been content with drinking the beverage. He brought back some of the pods and since, presumably, he still couldn't pronounce *tlilxochitl* he took the easy way out and called them *vanilla:* little pods. But the Spanish did more than give an imaginative name to the beans, they set up factories to make chocolate with a vanilla flavour. Soon, much of the continent was so hooked onto the taste of vanilla that they began to mix it with their tobacco. But for all the colonial might of the west, and the fact that they did succeed in persuading the vanilla plants to grow in Java, one of their tropical colonies in 1819, they just could not get them to fruit. For three centuries after Cortes and his conquerors drank *chocolatl,* Mexico continued to maintain its profitable monopoly of vanilla. This kept the Spanish happy, because Mexico was still their colony, but the other European powers gritted their teeth in rage.

Then, in 1836, a Belgian named Charles Morren discovered that this large problem was really a very minute one. It was a bee called *melipone* and a tiny humming bird which is almost as small as a bee. The vanilla flower had been so designed that there was a floral flap between the pollen-producing stamens and pollen-accepting stigmas of the flowers. Only the bees and the humming birds were equipped to penetrate this defence and pollinate the flowers of the vanilla. And only pollinated flowers produced pods. It was as simple and as frustrating as that: no bees and humming birds, no pods; no pods, no vanilla.

Enter the hero of the vanilla saga: a freed slave of the French possession of Reunion, an island in what is now the Republic of Seychelles. In 1841 this man, Edmond Albius, thought out of the box. He reasoned that what the bees

VANILLA

and humming birds could do with their tongues and beaks, he could do with a sliver of bamboo and his left thumb. Using the bamboo he raised the floral flap, called a restellum, took the sticky pollen grains from the stamens of the flower with his thumb and smeared it on the female stigma. Fertilisation complete, he moved on to the next flower. This is the simple, but delicate, process that is being used by vanilla farmers to this day.

Though, however, the process may seem simple, the vanilla orchid continues to make life difficult for its farmers. We learnt this on a visit to the Seychelles. Walking in a coconut grove in that island republic, we noticed that most of the trees were bright with the fleshy green leaves of a creeper. They looked a bit like pepper but were far more succulent. "These are vanilla vines," said our guide, "and those are the pods that eventually create the flavour that is so much in demand world-wide." He moved aside the leaves and showed us some of the bean-like fruit. "These are the pods and they are plucked when they are about five to ten inches in length but that isn't the end. It's a long, long process: both before and after that. It might be of interest to you, so you might like to speak to some experts about all that." We did, both in the Seychelles and in our own

A Vanilla vine

Left: Harvesting Vanilla pods

country, and we also read books about this delicately flavoured spice.

Briefly, the vanilla vine loves the moist tropics, well-drained soil rich in humus and needs the support of trees or trellises, like all creepers. Farmers plant cuttings at the base of their supports and encourage the vine to cling to them. If they are cosseted, and they need a lot of tender loving care, they should strike root in two-and-a-half to three months. Then for the next three years the vines have to be nurtured, protected from pests and predators, and pruned so that they do not grow out of the reach of their human pollinators. When the first pale yellow flowers bloom, the pollinators have to be quick off the

mark. Each blossom lasts from early morning to late afternoon and this is the only time when they can be pollinated. It takes another four to nine months for the pods to mature. They must be harvested just as they begin to turn from green to yellow, another *puff!-pant!* time for the anxious farmer.

That, however, is not the end of the process: far from it. Now starts the sweating and drying process. For ten to twenty days, the fruit of the vanilla vines, which look like beans, are exposed to the hot sun and then wrapped in blankets to sweat till the next morning. This is a natural fermentation process which speeds up the formation of a white crystalline substance known as *vanillin*. This is the real flavour of vanilla and there is no *vanillin* in the growing plant. In other words, there is no vanilla in vanilla: it has to be coaxed into existence!

Even when the *vanillin* appears the process does not end. The beans have then to be dried for many more weeks. In fact the whole process might take five to six months. A mechanical method has been developed to reduce this to a few days but that reduces the number of workers employed and so, often, efficiency gives

The drying of the beans

Methods of sweating and drying of Vanilla beans for sedimentation of white crystalline Vanillin on the beans. Vanilllin is the source of Vanilla essence the flavouring agent for ice-creams, cakes and other confectionery "

VANILLA

way to realpolitik! This artificial conflict cannot last for long because substitutes for vanilla have been developed from wood pulp, waste paper and even coal tar. But, according to the true connoisseurs of vanilla, there really is no substitute for the real thing. And as for introducing coal tar and waste into our Christmas delights all we can say is *Ugh!*

So, finally, we come to our last spice. It's popular, it's versatile and it is very easy

to grow. And if it didn't exist then a favourite American *timepass* would be monotonously tasteless.

Left: A close up of green Vanilla pods hanging down from the vine

Right: Vanilla pods hanging laid out to dry

It thrives in a tub in our lower garden.

No, it's not an aquatic, though one of its close relatives is. This zinc tub once belonged to a military ancestor and was described in the Army's records as:

> Tub, zinc: Officers, for the use of; with ears on the outside.

The 'ears' referred to the two handles on either side of the metal 'ablution equipment' and it was filled with the right amounts of hot and cold water by the unit bhisti. Rudyard Kipling wrote a poem about one of this tribe called Ganga Din. After many historic years of dedicated service, the tub began to leak so we relocated it to the garden, filled it with leaf-mould from our compost pit mixed with light, friable, soil from our oak wood,

and planted cuttings of *Mentha piperita* in it. All the cuttings struck root, in our temperate climate. Our garden gets a bit battered in our monsoon deluge and it withers if the frost bites it too viciously in the winter, but then we replenish the mint tub with fresh cuttings and it begins to thrive again. In fact the more leaf-bearing stems we snip off for the kitchen, the bushier the mint gets. We reward it, occasionally, by removing a little of the soil around the base of the plants and top-dressing it with fresh soil.

So much for the very easy cultivation of this rewarding pot herb.

This, probably, is what the Greeks and Romans did: pot gardens are still very

popular in all Mediterranean countries. As a sign of hospitality, the Greco-Romans would rub aromatic mint leaves on table tops to welcome their guests. We believe that this wasn't done merely to make their tables fragrant. We hang mint leaves in net bags in our kitchen and inquisitive insects stay away. This is, probably, also the reason why the ancient Jews spread mint leaves on their synagogue floors. Their places of worship would be both sweet smelling and pest free. Also pet free. Most dogs shun the smell of mint and refuse to curl up on even the softest of bedding if mint has been folded into it.

There were no dogs with the Roman legions as they conquered their way across the known world carrying their preference for mint with them. But although they had a garrison in their trading station of Muziris, in Kerala, mint does not seem to have become a popular spice in our southern states. In fact there appears to be a distinct *Lakshman Rekha*, a 'thus far and no further' line, stretching across the Vindhya Range. Mint is not a favoured culinary spice south of this line but fairly popular in North India.

In the great Gangetic Plain, and beyond, mint leaves add their green bite to the

Facing page: A sprig of Mint

Succulent Mint leaves

MINT

rich yoghurt drink *chaas* and, particularly in the winter, roadside *dhabas* produce the most mouth-watering mint, that is, *pudina*, parathas. *Pudina pakoras,* golden and sizzling hot from large cast-iron pans called *karais* are also a welcome snack for travellers on the misty northern roads. One reason for this North-South difference in the popularity of mint could be that southern dishes, with the exception of the cuisine influenced by Mughlai tastes, tend to be lighter than northern food and they have many more traditional digestives built into the meal. The north, being colder in winter, has developed more robust fare which takes longer to assimilate, and mint helps this process.

This presumption about the digestive qualities of Mint is reinforced by the way mint is used in English food. Traditionally, English fare was inclined to be stodgy and heavy. Diners needed something to stir their digestions and so, roast lamb was served with Mint Sauce or *Mint jelly*. It's easy to make *Mint Sauce.* Chop Mint leaves with sugar. Put the Mint and sugar into a sauce boat along with vinegar and water and allow it to stand for an hour before using it. Mint jelly is a little more complicated, but only a little. It calls for

boiling lemon juice, vinegar, sugar and mint leaves and then pouring in liquid pectin. Famed English chef, Philip Harben writes that *Mint Jelly* is 'a very agreeable accompaniment to Roast or Grilled Lamb or Mutton combining the agreeable qualities of mint sauce and red-currant jelly. It is a preserve which can be kept in store.' When *Mint Jelly* came to India, Anglo-Indian housewives added to the recipe, used gelatine instead of pectin, and converted it into a sandwich spread. But even with our fusion tastes in food, our community still treats mint as a garnish, a sauce or a spread, not as an essential part of the main meal. In his entertaining *The Raj at Table* author David Burton says, about 'chutneys made fresh each day:

> They are eaten as an accompaniment to rice and some not overly spicy meat or vegetable dishes.
>
> MRS. TEMPLE-WRIGHT'S FRESH CHUTNEYS. Mint Chutney
>
> One tablespoon of mint pounded to a paste, with lemon juice and a little salt, is very nice with cold meat.'

Mint chutney also refreshes both the tongue and the breath, as in fact all mints

A field of Mint: green as far as the eye can see. Inset is a close-up of Mint leaves, a favourite ingredient for fresh green chutneys and dips

Woman harvesting mint. Mint is one the easiest plants to grow and is popular as a pot plant or a house plant

MINT

do which is why both Peppermint and its relative, Spearmint, are popular flavours in chewing gum, popular with North Americans and people trying to give up smoking. Spearmint also goes into making a popular green liqueur: *Crème de Menthe*. In spite of its name, it contains no cream. It is, actually, a grape brandy in which Spearmint has either been gently boiled, called infusion, or in which the Spearmint has been soaked, or macerated. In both cases the object is to transfer the flavour of the Spearmint into the wine. Sugar is also added, the liquid is strained to remove any particles of Spearmint leaves, and colour added. It needs no brewing and a beer brewer has assured us that we can make it at home, 'Because absolutely no expertise is required.' We haven't tried but others undoubtedly have because the origins of this flavoured wine seem to go back into the distant past. Flavoured wines were popular with early tipplers and Spearmint is older than Peppermint. Some spice experts believe that Peppermint is a hybrid of Spearmint *(M. spicata)* and Watermint *(M. aquatica)* which we once saw growing in a stream in Kashmir's Gulmarg. Then there is Catmint which belongs to the same family, *Lamiasceae*, but not to the same genus Mentha. Its scientific name is *Nepeta cataria*. A pinch of its leaves

smelt, to us, like … well … dried leaves. But when the family cat, Francis, sniffed them he went berserk. He rolled on them and rubbed his face on them, all the while purring like a whirring dynamo. We wondered, then, if it has the same effect on all felines because, if it does, *Nepeta cataria* would be in great demand with guards in all the big cat sanctuaries of the world.

Finally, there's *Mentha arvensis* known as Japanese Mint because the industrious Japanese have large plantations of it. It is also grown in Uttar Pradesh, according to a friend who has made a study of spices. This Mint is not used directly to flavour foods but its aromatic, cool, product is Menthol, also known as Peppermint Camphor. It's not as strong as the oil extracted from Peppermint or Spearmint but there's more of it in this herb so it's cheaper to produce. It is also, according to the same well-informed friend, the spice product that earns the most revenue for our farmers. That, naturally, is a very sound reason for it to be smiled upon by the Spices Board, India.

That's *One* reason. But there are also many other *raisons d'etre*, important commercial and aesthetic reasons, for the existence of the Board.

The Reasons Why

SPICES BOARD INDIA

Kochi, a.k.a Cochin, is one of the most historic trading ports of the world.

Its beaches are washed by waves which have rolled in from Africa and the Persian Gulf. Across those waters of the Arabian Sea rowed the spice-questing boats of the Pharaohs, huge junks from Cathay cruising in from the South China Sea around the southern tip of our land, Roman galleons from the 'wine dark Mediterranean,' dhows from the Gulf driven by the monsoon, caravels from Portugal with painted sails and arrogant fidalgos, stocky Dutch carracks filled with sharp-eyed burghers, and East Indiamen from England with trade and acquisition in their hearts. They came powered by their desire to harvest the exotic flavours that grew in this rich coast.

The winds of history blew them in, and then blew them away but the green wealth of the land that had lured them, survived, in spite of its exploiters. And so when the land was returned to us, its people, we decided that it was time that we should help ourselves to enrich our green heritage.

We, the people of India, set up *Spices Board India* to *Discover, Propagate and Promote* the cause of Spices in all its facets. The emblem we chose for the Board was a sailing ship powered by the self-renewing forces of nature, seeking to push the frontiers of knowledge of this the greenest, most healthful, industry. It does not need belching smoke stacks or create enormous carbon footprints. It does not export the raw materials of our land. It does not scar the earth. Instead, it helps nature to create

Facing page:
Portuguese navigator, Vasco da Gama, pioneered Europe's spice-driven Age of Discovery. He was buried in Fort Cochin's Church of St. Francis.

In the contemplative light of dusk, the iconic Chinese Fishing Nets of Fort Cochin recall the arrival of bat-winged junks from distant Cathay, questing for Indian spices "

SPICES BOARD INDIA

its own value-addition in tiny, compact, packages which require little space and little energy to reach their consumers. The mission of this organisation was to unlock the secrets of these seeds and bark, bulbs, corms, pods and flowers into which nature had hidden untold treasures only hinted at by ancient, often, intuitive wisdom.

It would be difficult to think of a more relevant quest in our over-stressed world.

This early history of Indian spices has been expressed in the rolling phrases of a saga because that is what the story of spices, **Spicestory**, is. But though the role that spices have played in the development of our species, and the world in which we live, is an epic tale, the continuing activities of *Spices Board India* have to be told in more pragmatic, down-to-earth, terms.

And so, to today.

Reversing the track of the exploiters, our developers reached out, telling the world what we have and the terms on which they can share in our green wealth. Like the legendary *Starship Endeavour*, our spice pioneers voyaged to distant frontiers like Kiev in Ukraine and discovered that the Ukranians want a wide range of Indian

spices: turmeric, sesame, ginger, cumin, cinnamon and many others. In Paris our enquirers learnt that the French were interested in spice oils and oleoresins, and in black pepper, turmeric, mint and value added products like ginger and mint-flavoured candies, air fresheners and cosmetics blended with spice fragrances like vanilla and cinnamon. On the other side of the world in Parque Araucano, Santiago, Chile our representatives were asked about the rich flavours of our cumin, ginger, pepper and mint.

Encouraged by the interest that had been generated world-wide, the innovators of the Spices Board decided to host World Spice Congresses, inviting traders from other lands to visit India and meet the farmers of these very special little products. In 1990, when the first Congress was held in Bangalore, 78 foreign buyers came. This initiative burgeoned. When the 12th Congress was held in Kochi in 2014, there were over 300 of them from abroad.

Clearly the reach of Indian spices is growing. There are many reasons for this. The initial interest in Indian spices was generated by the descendants of Indians who had settled in the tropical colonies of the former British and French empires. In

Facing page: Map showing the Spice growing states of India

Spice Growing States of India

Jammu & Kashmir
Saffron
Ajowan
Ginger
Parsely
Chillies

Himachal Pradesh
Saffron
Ginger

Punjab
Celery
Aniseed

Utharanchal
Ginger
Chillies
Coriander
Aniseed

Haryana
Garlic

Rajasthan
Chillies
Coriander
Dill seed
Cumin
Fennel
Fenugreek
Mustard
Garlic

Uttar Pradesh
Mint, Turmeric, Chillies
Coriander, Fennel, Celery,
Fenugreek, Aniseed,
Garlic, Mustard,
Poppy seed

Gujarat
Chillies, Cumin
Fennel
Fenugreek
Garlic, Dill seed
Coriander

Madhya Pradesh
Coriander, Mustard
Fenugreek, Turmeric
Ginger, Chillies
Garlic, Poppy seed

Bihar
Turmeric
Parsely, Ajowan
Garlic
Mustard

Jharkhand
Ginger

Chhatisgarh
Garlic, Ginger
Turmeric

West Bengal
Cardamom (Large)
Ginger
Turmeric
Chillies

Orissa
Ginger
Turmeric
Chillies
Mustard

Maharashtra
Turmeric
Chillies, Garlic
Pomegranate seed
Nutmeg, Mace
Cambodge

Andhra Pradesh
Ginger
Turmeric
Chillies
Mustard
Tamarind

Karnataka
Pepper
Cardamom (small)
Ginger
Turmeric
Chillies, Clove
Nutmeg
Mace, Vanilla
Garlic
Kokkam
Cambodge

Tamil Nadu
Pepper
Cardamom (Small)
Ginger, Turmeric, Coriander
Clove, Nutmeg & Mace
Cinnamon & Cassia
Vanilla, Chillies
Pomegranate seed
Herbals
Exotic Spices

Kerala
Pepper
Cardamom (Small)
Chillies
Ginger, Turmeric
Clove,Nutmeg & Mace
Cinnamon & Cassia
Vanilla, Curry Leaf
Cambodge
Tamarind

Sikkim
Cardamom Large
Ginger
Tejpat

Arunachal Pradesh
Cardamom Large
Ginger
Turmeric, King Chillies
Star anise, Tejpat

Assam
Turmeric
Aniseed
Chillies

Meghalaya
Ginger
Turmeric

Nagaland
Cardamom Large
Ginger
Naga Chillies

Manipur
Ginger
Turmeric

Tripura
Turmeric
Pepper

Mizoram
Ginger
Turmeric

Leshadweep

Andaman Islands
Pepper
Cinnamon

स्पाइसेस बोर्ड
भारत
SPICES BOARD INDIA

SPICES BOARD INDIA

Sri Lanka, Malaysia, Singapore, Hong Kong, Mauritius, Seychelles and the West Indies. People of Indian Origin worked hard, rose to positions of authority and adapted their cuisines to their adopted environment. Hawkers' Stalls in the Straits sell variations of biryani, curries and the popular *Roti Canai*. In Mauritius they have even given French names to Indian kitchen equipment and condiments. Thus a *roche carri* is a masala stone, curry leaves are *carri poulle*, chutney has become *chatini* and *achar* is *achard*. Reflecting the French influence, which prefers slightly understated flavours, lemon, mango and palm heart go into their *achards*. Also adapting to the Gallic bias favouring the use of wines in cooking, the Mauritians often use rum as a flavouring agent sometimes super-charging it by marinating whole chillies in a half litre of the liquor for a fortnight.

Other historic conveyors of Indian cuisine were our ancient spice transporters, the Arabs. At one time their influence reached from the Gulf to North Africa, across much of the Iberian peninsula, impacted on their trading partners in

The allure of Indian spices is still being spread by traders, chefs and the diaspora. This is a restaurant in Singapore's Little India

Facing page: In Switzerland's Vevey, the owner of Poyet Confectionary is experimenting with spice-flavoured chocolates including one capturing the complex flavours of masala chai, spiced tea (left); Could the vitality of Indian children be explained by the energy-giving quality of spices? (right)

Turkey, Venice and Genoa from where it was dispersed across much of the rest of Europe, diminishing as it spread to the colder, northern, lands. We have visited thriving spice bazaars in Cairo, Aswan, Dubai, Aman and Istanbul and in Granada, facing the cathedral which was once a mosque, we stepped into an exceptionally well-stocked and well patronised spice shop. In Madrid we were introduced to a famed chocolate shop, where, among the many mouth-watering delights, they had a popular line of spice-flavoured chocolates.

All these testify to the long-lasting popularity of Indian spices in distant lands, but the world-wide demand for these condiments also got a major boost in the last quarter of the 20th century because

Cardamom
olate

Clove

Chocolates come
in a variety of
spices too

Clove
milk chocolate

Cumin

Chilly
milk chocolate

of the boom in travel and communications.

Thanks to the electronic revolution, the World Wide Web, satellite television and airlines crisscrossing the globe, the world is shrinking. More and more people are shedding their conservative lifestyles and experimenting with new cuisines. In a highly regarded chocolate boutique in Switzerland's Vevey, we met the owner of *Poyet Confectionary*. He had back-packed around India as a young man. He was so enchanted with the flavours of street-food in our land that he had created a chocolate that captures the taste of his favourite *masala chai* and another one in honour of His Holiness the Dalai Lama evocative of what he referred to … according to our interpreter … as 'Incense spices.' He said he was now working on a chocolate flavour that would capture the taste of 'those digestive after-meal seeds.' These innovations are symptomatic of the fact that Indian food is the cutting-edge flavour of the age, helped by our high-achieving Diaspora.

All these, however, are just opportunities and trends which would fade away when new interests grab the attention of our sensation-hungry generation. Exposure and availability are needed to stabilise a trend,

A gift box of chocolates flavoured with spices

and firm it into a tradition. Sometimes this happens by accident as in the case of the new British favourite: *Chicken Tikka Masala.* Legend has it that a group of British diners in an Indian restaurant in England sent back our traditional Chicken Tikka saying that it was too dry, too bland. "We didn't come here to have your Indian version of our cutlets. What's Indian about this?" An alert restaurant owner saw his main chance, recalled the dish, added Chicken Curry gravy and CTM was born. He saw the need, he added the available gravy, and a new tradition struck root.

Quick to respond to this growing global trend, the *Board* began to appear in international food festivals along with Indian chefs to show how simple it was to cook authentic Indian food using easily available Indian spices. Gradually the misconception that all Indian food is red, fiery and just curry-powder-stirred-into-stew, is being shredded. CTM made a dent in a conservative mindset; the *Board* enlarged that to a view of the wider horizons of our many cuisines.

Having spurred a demand for our spices, the *Board* set about demolishing another prejudice. Many Western spice dealers felt that the sources of even the most

delectable spices were suspect. They did not know where these condiments had come from, or if they could be sure of a continuing supply of them, or how safe they were. The formidable United States Food and Drug Administration, the USFDA, set daunting benchmarks for Traceability, Sustainability and Safety. Rather than dispute these standards, the Board decided to meet them.

Spice farmers were trained by spice exporting companies to meet the criteria demanded by importers. Such backward linkages were supported enthusiastically by farming groups particularly in Andhra, famed for the colour and quality of its chillies. It reached out to spice growers in Kerala and Tamil Nadu and to other spices like pepper, cardamom, cumin and coriander, turmeric, ginger, nutmeg and mace. As farmers learnt that their sales would soar when importers and consumers began to associate specific farmers, villages and certified processes with assured quality, they welcomed the *Board's* intervention.

Exporting companies who had their own certified laboratories, processing lines and packing facilities were awarded quality marks by the *Board.* There was a logo for consumer packs and another for the processor-exporter. Quality inspectors nominated by the *Board* make random checks to see that the standards required to use the logos are maintained at international levels. For those farmers who have not been able to tie up with certified processors, the *Board* has set up a prototype Spices Park in Kerala's Puttady with processing facilities on par with the most sophisticated in the world. Judging by the success of this venture other Spice Parks are likely to be established in many spice growing areas around India.

Then the *Board* took a major step to raise these efforts to an international level. In September 2012, the *Board* collaborated with the premier industrial body, the Confederation of Indian Industries, and the USFDA, to set up a training centre for food safety and supply chain management in Cochin.

The *Board* also reached down the supply chain to farmers located in areas far from major urban centres like Cochin. Tapping into India's incredible telecommunications boom, the *Board* has set up mobile tele-networks with another organisation, the IFFCO Kisan Sanchar Ltd, in spice-growing states in our country. Using this, farmers

The Spices Park at Puttady, the first such park developed by Spices Board in an area of ten acres, at Puttady in Idukki District of Kerala is meant for Cardamom (Small) and Pepper

SPICES BOARD INDIA

can have direct access to basic information, from the *Board,* including weather forecasts, spice cultivation, market trends and promotional activities. Moreover, not content with such electronic facilities, the *Board* has established direct person-to-person contact with spice farmers. Experts from the *Board* have fanned out to remote villages in our Sub-continental nation. In the village of Subhanidara, in the mountainous North-eastern state of Sikkim, specialists of the *Board* have helped increase both the productivity and the area under cultivation of the valuable Large Cardamom. Newly introduced methods of scientific curing have ensured better prices for spice farmers. Other innovations inspired by the *Board's* specialists have also brought better prices for turmeric for farmers in the village of Joma in the "Dawn state' of Arunachal Pradesh and for ginger in Parbuk village also in the North East. Technical innovations introduced by the *Board's* experts have won the admiration of major cardamom grower Paul Rai of Chisang village in West Bengal's Darjeeling district. "The large cardamom processed in the (*Board's*) bhatti are of good quality with fine colour and flavour," he said. From the other end of our land, Antu P.V. of Karukutty Edakunnu in Kerala praised the Board's innovative drier saying, "It is excellent!"

The *Board's* wide spectrum of activities extends from aiding such hands-on farmers to the ultimate arbiter of international food standards, world-wide. In Rome sits the impressively named Codex Alimentarius Commission established by the FAO and the WHO in 1963. The European Union and 185 countries participate in its deliberations. It lays down the international standards expected from all spices and herbs in their value-added forms including oils and oleoresins. On 5 July, 2013, on its 50th Anniversary in Rome, the Codex Alimenrtarius Commission accepted the proposal of the Board and formed a separate committee to handle Traceability, Sustainability and Food Safety exclusively for spices. This historic decision was taken in the 36th session of the Commission and it should ensure the standardisation of the quality of the increasing range and specialisations of spices and their many formulations, world-wide.

As we write this, there is a heavy blanket of snow in our garden. We've just phoned Dr PS Sreekantan Thampi, of the *Spices Board* in Cochin and asked him what the weather was like there, on the shores of the warm Arabian Sea. He said, "It's hot:

very hot!" That's one of the wonders of our country. It has snow and rain forests, deserts and great, dark, mangrove deltas, the highest mountains in the world, polder lands below sea level, saline scrub-plains and green coral islands. We can grow every spice that the world has ever known, and develop newer ones. We can also tap the vast reservoir of folk beliefs and old family traditions about the many benefits of spices. They are an integral part of the Indian way of life extending far beyond their use as flavouring agents. Traditional health and wellness practices laud the therapeutic virtues of our spices. During a long wait in Bahrain airport, we got into conversation with a man who said he was a nutritionist working with *Medicine Without Frontiers*, Before he left us he remarked: "My colleagues and I have often wondered why even the poorest, most deprived, children in India are so full of life. Perhaps, just perhaps, there are

components in your spices which interact directly with the mitochondria …!" Mitochondria in cells are structures responsible for energy and respiration.

We had entered this **Spicestory**, forty thousand years ago, speaking about an unknown spice discovered by a family of Neanderthals. There are still many unrecognised spices. We have seen them and tasted them in dishes cooked by our employee who is from a village deep in our mountains, and in sophisticated restaurants around the world where chefs guard them jealously. But there is no spice that we cannot grow. We must throw this as a challenge to the spice consumers of the world.

That is why we believe that the target of $ten billion in spices exports is well within the reach of the enterprising *Spices Board India.*

A Codex Alimentarius session in progress

Page 254-55:
Offices of the Spices
Board India

Epilogue
SPICE-ECHOES

Spicestory was a titanic symphony.

For many months we had had immersed ourselves in that great adventure of mankind, surging across the world, questing for spices. It had enthralled us, resonated within our lives. We were sad when it ended. But its echoes continued to ring softly, insistently, through the corridors of our minds.

We discovered this after we had sent the last chapter to the Spices Board, left our cottage in the oak woods of the Himalayas, and started our long drive to Delhi. Behind us, mist swirled through the trees, thunder growled and there was the chill bite of frost in the air. On the winding road down from the mountains, rain streaked in translucent tadpoles across the windscreen of our taxi, petering out as we reached the warmer plains. Golden fields of mustard spread on both sides of the highway, villages gave way to hamlets, towns grew, high-rises towered. We entered Delhi where the past and the present jostled for space.

Delhi lives in history, creates it, as it reaches out to the nations of the world, welcomes its citizens, shelters its diplomats.

The Diplomatic Enclave was green lawns, flowers and guarded embassies, each a little bit of a foreign land, asserting its distinct identity with its own architecture. The British High Commission was 4-square and very today, the Union Jack still flying bravely over the memories of an Empire on which the sun had finally set. The US Embassy was

Spices inspired
Hotel Ashok
to create these
innovative cocktails
and mocktails

SUMMER FUN

HOT PUNCH

a fantasy of glass and fret, architect Edward Stone's tribute to Old Delhi's Mughal heritage evoking the snide comment, *"People who live in Stone houses should always undress in the dark!"* The Americans gazed at the walled fastness of the embassy of the People's Republic of China: two great economic powers eyeing each other across an avenue in our burgeoning, bustling, land striving for its place in the sun. Then we swept up the drive of the great Ashok Hotel. Conceived by our first Prime Minister, Jawaharlal Nehru, crafted in a fusion of traditional architectural styles, this is Delhi's first, post-Independence, iconic structure proclaiming to the world the arrival of a new nation. Walking through the Ashok's gleaming halls and corridors graced with art, we thought we had left the old world behind. Surely this had nothing to do

SPICES-ECHOES

with the trials and tribulations, the intrigues and skulduggery of European traders scrambling for a share of the spices of the tropics. That belonged to a more grotty, more primitive, era. Or so we thought. But we were wrong. Spices have a dogged way of reaffirming their importance in all ages and in everything that humans do.

In the Ashok's *Frontier* and *Avadh* restaurants, catering to opinion makers in this magnetic hub of Asia, we discovered that they have created unusual drinks based not only on international wines and spirits but also on Indian spices. The echoes of *Spicestory* reverberated in our minds. We decided to investigate this new movement of the great spice symphony.

So one afternoon, when the Ashok's flock of white geese snoozed on the lawn outside the huge picture windows of one of the restaurants, we sipped, savoured, and extracted the secrets of the Ashok's spicy Mocktails and Cocktails with their evocative names which do not, necessarily, reflect their provenance.

The *Shaan-e-Oudh,* the Pride of Oudh, does not claim to be the original tipple of the very elegant, and reputedly sybaritic, nawabs of Avadh. Those princes of a state now absorbed into Uttar Pradesh had elevated social graces into such a fine art that they would make the perfumed dandies of the French Sun King's court look like red-necked boors. This mocktail is a mixture of guava juice, black pepper, black salt, lime juice and Limca. *Black Salt* is our term for rock salt which, according to ayurveda, is an effective aid to digestion. It goes well with the nip of pepper and, together, they give an appealing bite to the sweet blandness of the guava juice. This mocktail is a sophisticated version of a favourite snack of our childhood: the street vendors' wedges of guava spiced with black salt.

The aromatic black salt also dominates the *Noor-e-Oudh,* the Light of Oudh. This drink is reputedly as old as the Ashok though, if that is true, then the fizzy drink that is one of its principal ingredients seems to be a substitute for the British-era's Lemonade. The fact that this mocktail has the largest mixture of spices could account for its continuing popularity. Sprite is the base and into this goes roasted cumin seeds, lime juice and *chaat masala:* dried and powdered mango called *amchur,* cumin, dried ginger, black salt, coriander, asafoetida, pepper and red chilli powder. It comes in two strengths: the darker, and stronger, created in the *Frontier* restaurant, and also known as *Kala-*

Facing page:
Mocktails from Ashok: Shaan-e-Oudh, Noor-e-Oudh, Chashme Baddoor, Shatranj

Page 259: Ashok Hotel, New Delhi

SPICES - ECHOES

Noor, and the lighter, brown, one of the *Avadh*. As might be expected, they're both great mediators after a heavy meal!

In marked contrast is *Chashme Baddoor* literally Ward Off the Evil Eye. It is light and refreshing and, presumably, gives one a positive and cheerful mood disarming those with evil intentions. Its ingredients are fairly innocuous: grated cucumber, chopped ginger and mint, black pepper, black salt and ginger ale. The ginger ale gives character to the cucumber with the mint adding an attractive highlight. It's an attractive, undemanding, thirst quencher.

A shade more serious is *Shatranj* named after one of India's many gifts to the world, *Chess*. The nawabs of Oudh were said to be great chess players. This mocktail is a sort of fruity Bloody Mary with pineapple juice, orange juice, tomato juice, Worcestershire sauce, Tabasco sauce, lemon juice, white pepper and salt. Though the British claim that Worcestershire sauce was created in Worcestershire in 1843 we believe that it was based on an Indian sauce. Our family has a recipe for a sauce that is indistinguishable from Worcestershire though it does not have soy sauce as one of its ingredients as the British one does.

This brings us to the spicy, alcoholic, Cocktails. Two of them are served hot, and the other two cold; the hot ones have an Indian connection.

Hot Punch was, according to legend, created by pirates marauding in Indian waters. The word *Punch* is a corruption of our *Panch* because it originally had five ingredients. Rum, orange juice, cinnamon, cloves and sugar are the ones traditionally associated with *Punch*. From the 17th century onwards to the early 20th it was also a fairly common practice for the British and some other Europeans to sweeten, heat and spice their drinks, a process referred to as mulling, It is quite likely that this was done to ward of diseases fairly common in the unhygienic conditions of towns in the west. The Ashok's cocktail contains Bacardi Oro, cardamom, cinnamon, cloves, orange juice, a slice of orange and Lemon Zest.

The other hot cocktail is *Indian Grog*. This one has a naval background. It was the custom in Britain's Royal Navy to issue a tot of rum to all sailors. In the mid 18th century, however, Admiral Edward Vernon gave orders to dilute the sailors' ration with water. Since the greatly-disliked Admiral chose to wear a cloak made of

HOT PUNCH

THE ASHOK
New Delhi

INDIAN GROG

दि अशोक
THE ASHOK
New Delhi

SHATRANJ

दि अशोक
THE ASHOK
New Delhi

SPICES - ECHOES

the coarse textured grosgrain, he was known as *Old Grog* and the diluted drink became known as Grog. Today Grog is often served with hot water, lemon juice and sugar. The Ashok's Grog is more imaginative. It has Bacardi rum, cinnamon, black pepper, nutmeg and hot water. It is a great drink for a cold day, as we know from repeated personal experience.

Then, when the sun moves back towards the equator, *Summer Fun* is the answer. It has really cool flavours: vodka, sweet martini, mint leaf, lemon chunks, castor sugar, green chilli to give it that little kick, and soda. Lemon and mint are the flavours that remain in the memory with the green chilli squeaking its presence in a rather understated way. This is a friendly unassertive spice drink that hangs around and doesn't expect to be taken too seriously.

Finally, there's *Spice Surprise* which seems to be the younger sibling of Summer Fun, with attitude. Its citrus vodka gives it a younger image than the more sophisticated straight vodka and sweet martini. It also has lime juice, green chilli and Sprite. The reason why it is regarded as a cut above its kin is that it also has the world's most expensive spice: threads of saffron. One of us felt that the limey

flavours obscured the delicate taste of saffron; the other did appreciate the touch of that delicate flower-spice.

Our 21st century interest in spiced and hot drinks is an echo of the old mulled tradition. It could reflect a generational shift from hard spirits to more health-conscious drinks and lead to a demand for such mocktails and cocktails being factory blended and bottled. Crack the seal, mull or chill, pour, savour.

This thought struck us as we drove back from the Ashok to our Himalayan home. Then, a few days after we had settled in, we got a gift from the Spices Board. It was a box of bite-sized chocolates in six spice flavours. We recalled a chocolate shop in Madrid, and another in Switzerland, where they took pride in creating chocolates flavoured with spices. Those boutique products were meant for special occasions. So were these. They celebrated the 25th anniversary of the Spices Board and they came spiced with cardamom, cumin, clove, mace, cinnamon and chilli.

This is strictly in accordance with our Indian tradition which demands that when folks celebrate a great occasion, they are fed sweets by their relatives and friends.

Page 262-63: Hot punch Indian grog

Page 263: Shatranj

Which begs the question: *What will the Spices Board do to celebrate their next great achievement?* That's an easy one. This time they chose only six spices for their chocolates; we've written about eighteen of these flavoursome nuggets. Besides, there is the intriguing possibility of creating liqueur spice chocolates.

Clearly, there is no limit to the continuing echoes of the great symphony called the *Spicestory ....*

INDEX

INDEX